# Perspectives in Business Culture

For further volumes:
http://www.springer.com/series/10441

Antonio Borghesi · Barbara Gaudenzi

# Risk Management

## How to Assess, Transfer and Communicate Critical Risks

Springer

Antonio Borghesi
Department of Business Administration
University of Verona
Verona
Italy

Barbara Gaudenzi
Department of Business Administration
University of Verona
Verona
Italy

ISSN 2280-1464 ISSN 2280-2088 (electronic)
ISBN 978-88-470-2530-1 ISBN 978-88-470-2531-8 (eBook)
DOI 10.1007/978-88-470-2531-8
Springer Milan Heidelberg New York Dordrecht London

Library of Congress Control Number: 2012946753



Printed on acid-free paper

Springer is part of Springer Science+Business Media (www.springer.com)

# Preface

When I first met Antonio Borghese over 20 years ago I was impressed by his desire to share his knowledge and know-how on risk management and its role in our society. As we have often worked together since that first meeting I can attest that this desire has not diminished one bit and the following chapters demonstrate his desire to make the subject of enterprise risk management more accessible to both new and experienced practitioners alike. Antonio brings his ERM foresight into play by making this work available to a wider audience through this English version.

With the project leadership in the more than capable hands of Barbara Gaudenzi we have taken a systematic approach to presenting the key elements of enterprise-wide risk management concepts and actions.

It is essential to any person or organization engaged in the ERM process to begin with a well-founded understanding of the breadth and width of ERM practices. From a theoretical overview of ERM, the establishment of a common language and standard to a clear analysis of alternative risk financing mechanisms, this work will allow the reader to grasp both the basic concepts and the more advanced thoughts around ERM.

The interconnectedness of risk even in the most diverse organizational activities and the need to keep a competitive edge in today's marketplace make this work a must read for all levels of management.

We trust that you will gain valuable insight and a shared vision of why ERM is an essential ingredient of a well-managed and sustainable organization.

Tony Cabot
Director Product Development for Europe and Asia, Argo Group
Senior Executive Officer, Argo Re (DIFC) Ltd.

# Contents

## Part IV Supply Chain Risk Management and Business Continuity

# Part I
# Reference Theories

# Chapter 1
# From Social and Natural Science Comes a Historical Overview on the Concepts of Uncertainty and Risk

## 1.1 Risk… Beginning with Newton and Heisenberg

Whomever is interested in understanding the concept of risk and its interpretation should consider some important reflections provided by the principles of the theories of physics, from pure physics to Newtonian theories.

In the works *The method is the ideology: from a Newtonian to a Heisenbergian paradigm in economics* and *reflections on uncertainty in economics,* Weisskopf (1979) describes the *cognitive aspect* (which endeavors to provide an explanation on the unknown) and the *regulatory aspect* (aimed at outlining lines of action and behaviors for the individual) of human actions.

These and the following reflections are particularly important in studying risk management.

Among the emblematic paradigms from a cognitive point of view, the following are noteworthy:

- *Newton's or celestial mechanics paradigm.* This states that reality is independent from the observer: subject and object belong to separate and distinct spheres. Moreover, it highlights how, once the system's instantaneous state has been identified, its future evolution is also determined.
- *Heisenberg's or the indetermination paradigm.* Following many intuitions and discoveries in different spheres of science, it is mainly the emerging science of thermodynamics that makes an important breakthrough in classical mechanics, by proving—thanks to Boltzmann—*the existence in nature of irreversible processes* and describing entropy as the extent of the spontaneous evolution of an isolated system toward its state of thermodynamic balance. It is in this context that *for the first time probability is introduced in physics to explain a phenomenon rather than approximate it.* This turning point is indeed essential for risk analysis. The most important turning point for a total break from the past, was reached by Heisenberg and his indetermination (or uncertainty) principle, which crossed quantum mechanics. Heisenberg reverses the supposition of the separation between observer and object being observed, stating that

A. Borghesi and B. Gaudenzi, *Risk Management*, Perspectives in Business Culture,
DOI: 10.1007/978-88-470-2531-8_1, © Springer-Verlag Italia 2013

the influence of the observer on the position and speed of the particles makes it impossible to know both of them at the same time. *The observer changes the image of reality and becomes one and the same with the object*. These reflections are important for understanding the weight of subjectivity in risk assessment.

- Prigogine's or dissipation structures paradigm. If classical thermodynamics show that a system in a situation of non-balance drifts toward balance, Prigogine's paradigm proves that, in living creatures, few are the processes that move toward the situation of balance and that there are many cases where the state of non-balance generates structures that are evolving toward states of "orderly complexity". This paradigm raises uncertainty as the engine room of the lives and actions of living creatures.

It is in the areas of high improbability—almost in agreement with Popper's (1959) theories—that we can find the answer to the reality surrounding us. Minor fluctuations around the stationary condition are reabsorbed by the system, but when they amplify beyond a certain limit *the system becomes unstable and this instability generates a morphological transformation* that makes it evolve toward a new order.

## 1.2 Uncertainty and Risk: Loss and Gain—A Historical View

Since the eighteenth century, thanks to Smith (1776), the concept of risk is mainly linked to the concept of unfavorable event. An exception is represented by Smith, who did not comprehend risk in his studies.

In the twentieth century, mainly in the U.S., we had the first instances of risk in the business sphere being dealt with for the purpose of identifying techniques and procedures for the identification, measurement, and treatment of risk in business decisions.

At the beginning of the twentieth century, the first significant studies in business risk management were developed by Willet (1901), Leitner (1915), Knight (1921), Oberparletier (1930), Stadler (1932), and Sassi (1940). These authors for the first time treated risk as an independent topic of study, and described 'risk' as a measurable uncertainty in contrast with the concept of non-measurable uncertainty (ignorance about future events).

Between the two world wars the Austrian (Viennese) school and the Italian school (from Florence) were the most relevant ones in Europe, particularly with Oberparleiter, Leitner, Corsani, and Fazzi.

Worthy of a brief comment are the reflections developed by Rowe (1977) and later by Borghesi (1979) when the latter describes the concept of uncertainty as "the lack of information on parts of a system under consideration" which may be expressed on a scale from 0 (certainty) to 1 (total uncertainty). The absence of information required to describe the system brings about a situation of *descriptive uncertainty*, whereas the lack of information required to measure variables, brings about a situation of *measurement uncertainty*.

A feature that is common to the management of systems and related processes is represented by the consequences that may be alternatively either losses or gains, where, in the presence of competitors, the loss by one entity may be conversely the gain by another. Risk therefore appears to be associated with consequences that involve losses for those who take it. Risk agents often voluntarily expose themselves to risks in order to achieve possible gains if the possible gains exceed possible losses. If, instead of "possible" gains and losses we were to refer to "probable" gains and losses, their quantitative balancing is possible within the limits of measurement uncertainty. On these grounds, we must associate risk to losses alone; in other words, let us assume that Man is opposed to risk. At any rate, we have risks that at times are taken to achieve possible desired gains. The action undertaken to reduce the risk may be considered a gain in the sense that a possible loss is reduced.

This, in summary, is Rowe's opinion, who concludes by defining risk as "the realisation potential for undesired and negative consequences of an event".

Even though this has been for a long time the prevailing position, other authors have defined the risk by distinguishing the dual character of risks capable of producing alternatively either losses or gains, for example through choices and events that have financial consequences. See, for example, Mowbray et al. (1979), Dickinson (2001), Bannister et al. (1981) and Carter (1979).

According to this position, indeed, it is impossible to see what logical difference may be found between the situation where an individual, due to the occurrence of a certain event, suffers a loss or a smaller gain compared to the one expected.

Two examples. Let us assume the case of a business that has forecast in the production planning an "equipment failure" equal to 5 % of hours worked. The "equipment failure" may be certainly classified among the unfavorable events. Let us now assume, in hindsight, that the equipment failure that has actually occurred is equal to 3 % of hours worked. Certainly this is not an unfavorable event: so long as the "equipment failure" remains below the planned 5 % we can only maintain that for this business, the event was favorable, being equal to the difference between the planned and the actual rates.

Now let us assume that an economic initiative whereby a profit of 1000 had been forecast and that, in hindsight, recorded instead an actual profit of 500. The profit of an economic initiative is by definition a favorable event. However, the businessmen will maintain that an unfavorable event has occurred with an effect equal to the difference between the forecast figure and the figure actually recorded.

From the above considerations we can conclude that, depending on the position of the entity concerned, an unfavorable event may turn into a favorable event, and vice versa.

Indeed, it is our opinion that the attempt to objectivise concepts such as the concept of risk (or the concept of a favorable or unfavorable event) clashes with the dominant logics of relativism. It is also amazing that, while social science has over the past century pursued objectivity in their theories, natural science, at the same time, has partially reversed this approach (Prigogine et al. 1984; Giarini 1981).

The conceptualization of risk cannot but undergo a review of the concepts of favorable and unfavorable events, based on the acknowledgement of their dynamic, subjective, and ambivalent character.

Therefore, we will describe as *unfavorable event the negative sign deviation from a given expected situation*. Conversely, a favorable event will be a deviation of the opposite sign.

These concepts are today basically adopted within an international and segmented view, especially by ISO.

In 2009, ISO, through **ISO Guide 73: 2009**, led to the definitions of generic terms related to risk management.

In that Guide **risk is defined as the "effect of uncertainty on objectives".**

Guide 73 also states that an effect may be positive, negative, or a deviation from the expected, and that risk is often described by an event, a change in circumstances or a consequence.

This definition links risks to objectives. Therefore, this definition of risk can most easily be applied when the objectives of the organization are comprehensive and fully stated.

The consequences of a risk may be either negative (hazard risks), or positive (opportunity risks), or could lead to uncertainty.

"Hazard" includes the hazardous event and its negative consequences, as well as the causes behind that event. Hazards are traditionally divided into natural hazards (like earthquakes and hurricanes), social, and moral hazard (like terrorism and theft) (Pidgeon et al. 1992).

Uncertainty is *the lack (even if only partial) of information about a future situation (or state of a system).*

When the event through its occurrence impacts on a relationship situation, the sign deviation will be measurable mainly in qualitative terms, whereas in the case of an economic-financial situation (irrespective of whether it is personal or corporate) the sign deviation will be measurable mainly in quantitative terms.

The concept of risk also has an ambivalent nature, where, as stressed by Rowe, "the loss by an individual may be the gain by another". While this may be true in the case of two gamblers playing against each other, where it is clear that the gain by one player corresponds to a loss by another, this can also be found in socio-economic contexts, such as the running of a business.

In view of the above definitions of risk and uncertainty, it is worthwhile pointing out the difference between them and introduce the concept of *peril,* which may be defined as the cause or source of the unfavorable event. As an example, perils are fire, earthquakes, car collisions, sabotage, and so forth.

Instead we call *hazard* the condition/s that may create or increase the likelihood of the occurrence of an unfavorable event arising from a given peril. In general we identify three major classes of hazards:

- Physical hazards: objective factors capable of increasing the probabilities of the unfavorable event (e.g., the presence of ice on the road, the presence of flammable materials in a warehouse, etc.).
- Moral hazards: dishonesty or character flaws of an individual that increase the likelihood of the unfavorable event (e.g., an individual insured against fires who, finding himself in financial hardship, deliberately sets fire to the insured property).
- "Morale hazard": a situation of carelessness, negligence, dereliction of duty, indifference faced with danger.

## 1.3 The First Risk Classifications

Major advancement in the study of risk in business theory took place in the period between the two world wars in Europe (especially Italy and Germany) and the U.S.

There have been many risk classifications that have been put forward in the managerial literature and practice. The most important of them are discussed herein, while leaving to later chapters the analysis of the different types:

1. Risks classified based on the **effects resulting from the event occurrence**. On this basis, we would distinguish between *economic risks and non-economic risks*. The former would be susceptible to causing monetary losses, while the latter would be susceptible to causing non-monetary losses.
2. Risks classified based on the **criterion of the nature or origin of the potentially unfavorable event**. On the basis of this criterion, risks have been distinguished by some as *technical and economic*. The former would be linked to the use of production technology while the latter would be more strictly associated with the economic-business activity (such as the failure to sell products despite their being technically perfect). Drucker, based on the same criterion, distinguished between *physical risks and economic risks*: the former due to improper actions of physical and natural forces, the latter associated with Man's economic activities. Oberparleiter has further distinguished the economic risks into social, natural, commercial subjective (i.e., specific to the entrepreneur) and commercial objective (i.e., specific to the product).
3. **Static risks and dynamic risks**. The former are linked to losses caused by the improper action of nature and errors and misunderstandings by human beings. The latter are associated with economic changes, especially in human needs and technological and organizational improvements.
4. Risks classified based on the **type or nature of the economic result resulting from the event.** They are broken down as follows:

   - property risks: these relate to the destruction, damage, disappearance of the property with resulting costs and loss of earnings;

- liability risks: events entailing a legal liability;
- personal risks: events involving physical risks for people.

5. **Pure risks from speculative risks**. Pure risks are all those earlier identified as property, liability, and personal risks. Speculative risks are encountered on a daily basis in most business decisions: for instance, the extension of a factory may create earnings but also losses.

However, further classifications are possible, if they contribute to more effective risk assessment and treatment processes.

## References


Bannister JE, Bawcutt PA (1981) Practical risk management. Witherby, London

Borghesi A (1979) Rischio aziendale, risk management e strategia delle imprese di assicurazione. Il Risparmio No.9/1979

Carter RL (1979) Economics and insurance. PH Press, Stockport

Dickinson G (2001) Concepts of probability and risk, handbook of risk management. Kluwer-Harrap Handbooks, London, pp 1974–1984

Giarini O (1981) Some considerations on the activity of insurance business and its relevance for a general re-assessment of economic theory. Geneva Papers , No. 21, p 90

Knight F (1921) Risk, uncertainty and profit. Chicago University Press, Chicago

Leitner F (1915) Die Unternehmengsrisiken, Berlino

Mowbray AM, Blanchard RH, Williams CA (1979) Insurance. Krieger Publishing Co., Huntington (original edition by Mowbray 1930)

Oberparleiter K (1930) Funktionen und Risiken des Warenhandels. Springer, Wien

Pidgeon N, Hood C, Jones D, Turner B (1992) Risk perception In: risk: analysis, perception and management. The Royal Society, London

Popper K (1959) The logic of scientific discovery. Hutchinson, London

Prigogine Y, Stengers I (1984) Order out of Chaos. University of Michigan, Bantam Books, New York

Rowe WD (1977) An anatomy of risk. Wiley, New York

Sassi A (1940) Il sistema dei rischi di impresa. Vallardi, Milano

Smith A (1776) An inquiry into the nature and causes of the wealth of nations. Strahan Ed., London

Stadler M (1932) Studien aus der Theorie des Risikos. Institut für Welthandelslehre, Wien

Weisskopf WA (1979) The method is the ideology: from a Newtonian to a Heisenbergian paradigm in economics. J Econ Issue, No. 13

Willet A (1901) The economic theory of risk and insurance. Philadelphia University Press, Philadelphia

# Chapter 2
# Governance and Risk Management

## 2.1 Three Interpretative Models: The Paradigm of "Structure-Conduct-Performance", "System Theory", and "Value-Based Management"

For the purpose of defining the risk management action area, three important managerial analysis models are:

- structure-conduct-performance paradigm and the functional view of risk management;
- systemic approach and transversal/process view of (risk) management;
- value-based management and value perspective.

### *2.1.1 The North-American School and the Structure-Conduct-Performance Paradigm*

Until the 1960s, in North America the environmental and competitive context was such as to reward the large multi-division business model: just think of General Motors, Standard Oil or Du Pont, which embodied managerial best practices and where the greatest management thinkers of that period operated (e.g., Alfred Sloan and Peter Drucker in General Motors).

In this context, managerial studies focused mainly on the ability to harmonize the "forecast, planning, organization, control, coordination and monitoring" moments which were the foundations of the managerial paradigm of *structure-conduct-performance* (Ansoff 1965; Drucker 1946). According to Chandler's and Galbraith's theories, whereby "structure should follow strategy", the strategic development decisions, such as, for example, vertical integration or diversification, should be made through centralized planning capable of "guiding" the restructuring of the organization. Only a few years later, Schumacher began to observe that every multi-division structure, such as General Motors, in fact would resemble

A. Borghesi and B. Gaudenzi, *Risk Management*, Perspectives in Business Culture,
DOI: 10.1007/978-88-470-2531-8_2, © Springer-Verlag Italia 2013

a "federation of reasonably large businesses": here Schumacher was perhaps the first exponent of a new current of thought that gave small business a positive connotation for business competitiveness (Schumacher 1973).

This model focused on individual organizations, governed by the principles of an infallible *scientific management* capable of ensuring a "natural" balance, according to Fayol's description, between strategic planning and its implementation at all levels of the organization (Drucker 1974; Chandler 1962, 1977; Fayol 1949; Taylor 1947).

This cultural and managerial context gave rise to the early approaches to risk management as planning and implementation of risk control techniques through, typically, the tool of insurance transfer. Indeed it is in this managerial context that Mowbray et al. (1979), some years later, also distinguished the concepts of *speculative risk and pure risk, which were briefly introduced in the previous chapter* (Carter and Doherty 1984; Giarini 1982):

1. *The speculative risks* are those that can generate alternatively, either gains or losses. In this context we can refer to risks linked to financial management and strategic choices associated with the business activity, which are capable of generating profits, but also conversely, losses. We can think, for example, of risks linked to events and choices such as production delocalization, changes in the structure of production costs or loans, the failure of new technologies or new products, the reduction in sales or market share, competitors' actions, or, in general, socio-cultural, political or regulatory changes.
2. *The pure risks* are those that can generate only losses. We can name for example: interruptions, failures, or breakdowns of production equipment; thefts, fraud or other malicious acts; catastrophes; accidents to people, illnesses or death.

In this economic and social context there developed, as we will see later, the **functional approach** to risk management, based typically on insurance products.

### 2.1.2 Business as an Open System and the Systemic Approach to Business Governance

Among the founders of the systemic approach we should first mention Emery (1969) and the biologist Ludwig von Bertalanffy (1969) who analyzed and embodied the different approaches to the systems theory (in the subjects of biology, physics, sociology, economics, and business organization), and described the open and closed systems in relation to the environment as well as their respective operational dynamics.

This line of thought highlights the systemic nature of a business, meaning that each organization represents a "system" belonging to others and in turn is made up of sub-systems, thus developing an intrinsic synergy.

From this we can draw the **following principles**:

- organizations belong to larger systems that encompass them, such as, for example, the reference environment or–from other perspectives–the sector, district, industry or value chain;
- organizations include internal sub-systems such as decision-making units, functions and processes;
- the organizational structure of a corporation is expressed by its network of internal and external interactions.

The environmental changes that occurred during the 1970s and 1980s impacted to a significant extent on the features and nature of demand, production processes and competition dynamics. All this has entailed for businesses the need to confront themselves with a significant evolution of the "parameters" of excellence and competitiveness (Peters et al. 1982; Peters 1987; Mintzberg 1989), thus highlighting the need to review and transform the rigid hierarchical/top-down, yet transversal structure (from which the identification and management process of the distinctive skills should stem).

This economic and social context witnessed the consolidation, as we will see later, of the **transversal approach** to risk management, based on risk identification, assessment and treatment tools which, rather than being only insurance-based, were drawn from different business environments (Committee of Sponsoring Organizations of the Treadway Commission (COSO) 2002–2004).

### *2.1.3 Value-Based Management*

Value Based Management (VBM) is the management approach that ensures that corporations are run consistently on value (normally: maximizing shareholder value).

The three basic elements of VBM are:

1. VBM is permeated by the principle that value creation is the primary aim of the business;
2. VBM means making decisions, allocating resources, remunerating management with the aim of creating value. The ultimate purpose is to make sure that at each level of the organization, management is encouraged to act as if it were the owner of the business;
3. VBM is a tool for assessing the success or failure of the management activities that are in their inception phase or that are being implemented. VBM is a tool for anticipating what contribution a certain activity will be able to make to value creation.

The main feature of Value-Based Management is that all the decision-making processes, planning, and the control systems are strictly related to the objective of maximizing value creation for the shareholders.

Managing with a view to creating value begins with the strategy and ends with the financial results: Management is responsible for creating the link between strategy and results. The mission of every business is to create value. This new imperative gives rise to strategies, organizational models and new management systems that, considered as a whole, give rise to the concept of Value-Based Management.

This vision is an essential contribution for interpreting the Risk Management process, whose objective is indeed **the protection of the business from unfavorable events in order to maximize its value creation capacity**.

## 2.2 Governance and Value Creation

Consistently with the systemic view of the business and the VBM, the body charged with the governance has the task of setting up and guiding development actions, i.e., the system evolution dynamics. Furthermore it develops the coordination of and with the sub-systems, as it is responsible for both ensuring the economic objective of maximizing value creation and complying with a "social task": the balance of interests and the social legitimization with and from various public reference models.

In the current environmental context, the roles of the governance body and the boundaries of governance change: the push from globalization leads to competition among business networks and no longer between individual businesses; the competition excellence levers are increasingly reaction speed and innovation (time) and the optimization of the cost/quality ratio of the product/service. The need to simultaneously manage diverse and at times opposing strategic objectives encourages businesses to take on increasingly greater levels of risk. Therefore, the conditions of riskiness are linked to both the environmental context and the strategic and managerial choices made by businesses.

Stakeholders have more and more access to information and demand greater transparency and responsibility from businesses. For these reasons the role of compliance has increased significantly in importance. This role includes compliance with regulations and the proper disclosure of corporate choices to stakeholders.

To this end the Corporate Governance system should introduce voluntary rules (codes of conducts and self-regulations, resulting from the internal control system) or a systematic approach to monitoring compliance with the rules.

The purpose is to ensure:

- "compliance" with binding regulations;
- "communication" to and with stakeholders;
- "assurance" regarding risk tolerance;
- decision-making, efficacy of the strategy and efficiency of operations.

In this regard, we note that where there is a need for so-called "global" governance models, for example for businesses operating on international markets, the risk management models become more complex.

**Table 2.1** The potential value of a business

| | | | |
|---|---|---|---|
| Potential value of the business | Economic capital value | ROE | Tax planning<br>ROI<br>Leverage |
| | | CAPITAL INVESTED<br>Duration of expected normal average income<br>Capitalization rate | |
| | Growth opportunities value | Development rate | Internal (dividends policy)<br>External (financial policy)<br>Sales —market shares<br>Purchases |
| | | Duration of competitive edge<br>Profit rate (expected ROE) | |

The "global" Governance should extend its competency to the following dimensions (Brawn et al. 2004):

- internal dimension (employees);
- networking dimension (co-makers and partners);
- integration dimension (global market);
- transparency dimension (shareholders and finance);
- corporate ethics dimension (government and media).

Therefore, the purpose of the corporate governance system is not only to support value creation but also to manage stable and durable relationships with the stakeholders. The value levers can be broken down into capital profitability levers and value levers linked to competitive edge, which measures the growth and development opportunities over time (Table 2.1).

A closer look shows the ability to manage such relationships represents a tool, if not an essential condition, for the purpose of gaining a solid reputation and therefore maintaining profitability over time.

As a result, the organization must manage those risks that may impair the value of the business, focusing in particular on the following aspects:

- Long-term perspective: the risk must be managed with long-term strategies and approaches, because competitive edge and value consolidate in the long term;
- systematic risk: risk management will need to integrate the value creation perspectives:
  - "macro" risks: linked to global, EU, domestic and industry-specific factors;
  - "micro" risks: linked to the strategic and tactical choices made by individual businesses.

It should be noted that the measurement of the value of the business is traditionally based on financial, income-related and asset-related methods. The risk analysis is also based on similar methods. Are we really capable of measuring the competitive advantage and its vulnerability by using only these approaches? Managers should always analyze in detail the most appropriate and effective tools.

## 2.3 Corporate Governance: Regulatory Evolutions

The recent evolutions in the legislative and socio-economic framework have set up a new scenario for risk management. In the various countries, legislators, international bodies, and supervisory bodies have made regulations ever more stringent.

The promulgation of laws and rules that impose on companies stringent obligations relating to governance principles and procedures has stimulated investment growth of businesses through integrated risk management approaches, aimed at ensuring a better control and protecting themselves from the risk of non-compliance. We wish to briefly mention some of the more effective initiatives, albeit bearing in mind that there are many developments under way:

- the Sarbanes–Oxley Act, issued on July 30th, 2002 in the U.S., represents the reform legislation for the corporate governance system of companies listed on the U.S. Stock Exchange for the purpose of protecting investors by improving the accuracy and reliability of corporate information;
- the Combined Code on Corporate Governance, United States, 2003, new version in 2006;
- the Turnbull Guidance, United Kingdom, 1999, and subsequent Smith Guidance and Higgs Guidance;
- Government White Paper, modernizing Company Law, European Commission, 2003;
- Federal Complementary Act to the Swiss Civil Code, "Obligations Code" chapter, 2008.

Significant have been the impacts of the Sarbanes–Oxley Act issued in the United States not so much for the purpose of providing best practice on the governance principles but rather for the purpose of imposing a clear and stringent business liability regime and raise the level of "criminal penalties".[1] It is not by chance that it was issued after the Enron and Worldcom scandals. Still in the United States, similar to the Sarbanes–Oxley Act is the Combined Code on Corporate Governance, published in 2003 and updated as early as in 2006 as a review of the first version published in 1998 by the Financial Reporting Council. The Combined Code does not have the force of law, but it purports to be a codification of the corporate governance principles. Overall, there are 17 of them, from which businesses should draw inspiration.

Unlike in the United States, in other countries, especially the United Kingdom, guidelines on corporate governance have been issued for the purpose of introducing exemplary best practices in order to encourage imitation. The Turnbull Guidance

[1] It is estimated that some 60 % of large US businesses, with a turnover of 20 billion dollars or more, have invested the equivalent of 100,000 man hours (comparable to the full time employment of 70 people for one year) in order to comply with the compliance obligations set, in particular, by Section 404 of the Sarbanes–Oxley Act.

issued by Chartered Accountants in England and Wales and the subsequent Smith Guidance and Higgs Guidance had the initial aim of introducing some guidelines on the implementation of the internal audit section of the Combined Code, and later extending to the areas of corporate governance without ever acquiring the force of law.

Also a Government White Paper, titled "Modernizing Company Law", was issued by the European Commission in 2003 not for the purpose of defining a single corporate governance code at European level, but rather to introduce a common approach to some essential aspects.

Moreover, in 2008, some amendments were made to the Federal Complementary Act to the Swiss Civil Code, "Obligations Code", that impose on all companies subject to standard audits the obligation of setting up a formal internal audit system, and, on auditing firms, the obligation of certifying the existence of such a system and taking this into account in their auditing work.

In Italy, for example, the main reference legislation on the subject of controls was introduced from 1997 to 2001:

- Legislative Decree No. 231 of June 8th, 2001, containing "Rules on the administrative liability of corporations", introduced for the first time, in our legal system, criminal liability of Companies and their directors for certain types of offenses, especially those against the Public Administration;
- Law No. 262/2005, introduced a number of new provisions on the subject of governance of Italian companies. In particular it introduced provisions on the subject of liability and obligations relating to corporate disclosures (similarly to the provisions of Sections 302 and 404 of the U.S. Sarbanes–Oxley Act of 2002);
- Consob Recommendations (Memo of February 20th, 1997) on the subject of corporate control;
- Finance Consolidated Act (Legislative Decree No. 58/1998), which establishes the duties of Statutory Auditors on the subject of supervision and internal audit;
- Code of Conduct of the Italian Stock Exchange;
- Instructions by Bank of Italy regarding the Internal Controls System;
- Legislative Decree No. 231 of June 8th, 2001 (as amended) on the subject of Companies' Administrative Liability.

In addition to the laws and guidance statements directly linked to the issues of governance, reference can be made to many other areas of legislative applications that affect, to a significant extent, the governance system, for instance:

- directors' liability;
- business continuity and disaster recovery;
- safety and security;
- environmental regulations.

The Organization for Economic Co-operation and Development (OECD) has provided a definition of the contents of *Corporate Governance*,[2] that highlights, in particular:

- Board of Directors' liability;
- commitment to an effective corporate governance;
- the role of stakeholders and the commitment to the utmost disclosure and transparency;
- fair treatment of shareholders.

Therefore, Corporate Governance extends beyond the area of relationships with shareholders only, based on the *agency theory* or *shareholder value theory*) (Fama et al. 1983), and affects all stakeholders in their capacity as parties responsible for the social legitimization of the company. It should be stressed in no uncertain terms that the significant focus on social legitimization resulting from the many stakeholders represents one of the reasons why today reputational risk management is so important, as we will see in next chapters.

The Sarbanes–Oxley Act entailed the establishment of the Public Company Accounting Oversight Board (PCAOB), with the task of defining the Auditing Standards, by Management, of the internal control system.

The PCAOB Auditing Standard No. 2. para. 14 reads as follows:

> In the United States, the Committee of Sponsoring Organizations (COSO) of the Treadway Commission has published Internal Control–Integrated Framework. Known as the COSO report, it provides a suitable and available framework for purposes of management's assessment.

The COSO Report is therefore the framework better known and accredited for implementing governance.

As we will see later, it is yet to be proven that it represents the best approach to risk management.

Risk management and Internal control should coexist but are not the substitutive. The Internal Control System represents a set of rules, procedures and organizational structures aimed at ensuring:

- compliance with corporate strategies;
- achievement of the effectiveness and efficiency of corporate processes;
- safeguard of the value of the activities and protection from losses;
- reliability and integrity of accounting and management information;
- operational compliance with laws and regulations.

The risk assessment is part of the internal control activities, but does not end there. This means that not all the risk assessment approaches and techniques can be managed and governed by the internal control manager.

---

[2] In 1999 the Corporate Governance Principles were approved, on the request of the OECD Council of Ministers (later updated in 2002). The World Bank, the International Regulations Bank and the International Monetary Fund took part in the process as observers.

## References


Ansoff HI (1965) Corporate strategy. McGraw-Hill, New York

Brawn L, Caylor M (2004) The correlation between corporate governance and company performance. Institutional Shareholders Services, No. 31

Carter RL, Doherty NA (1984) The development and scope of risk management. In: Handbook of risk management. Kluwer-Harrap Handbooks, New York, pp 1–11

Chandler AD (1962) Strategy and structure. MIT Press, New York

Chandler AD (1977) The Visible hand: the managerial revolution in American business. Harvard University Press, New York

Committee of Sponsoring Organizations of the Treadway Commission (COSO) (2002–2004), Internal control-integrated framework (ICIF). www.erm.coso.org,

Drucker PF (1946) Concept of Corporation. John Day, New York

Drucker PF (1974) Management: tasks responsibilities practices. Heinemann-Harper and Row, New York

Emery FE (1969) Systems thinking. Penguin Books, Harmondsworth

Fama EF, Jensen MC (1983) Separation of ownership and control. J Law Econ 26(2):301–325

Fayol H (1949) General and industrial management. Pitman and Sons, London (first edition-1938)

Giarini O (1982) «Développement économique et croissance des risques». Geneva Papers, (22):19

Mintzberg H (1989) Mintzberg on management. The Free Press, New York

Mowbray AM, Blanchard RH, Williams CA (1979) Insurance. Krieger Publishing Co, Huntington

Peters T (1987) Thriving on chaos. Alfred A. Knopf, New York

Peters T Jr, Waterman RH (1982) In search of excellence. Harper and Row, New York

Schumacher EF (1973) Small is beautiful. Blond and Briggs, London

Taylor FW (1947) Scientific management. Harper and Row, New York (first edition of 1912)

Von Bertalanffy L (1969) General system theory: foundations, development, applications. George Braziller, New York

# Chapter 3
# Risk Management Perspectives

## 3.1 Risk is Transversal

"Risk" cannot be eliminated. Organizations therefore need to manage all the factors that increase and reduce those risks so that they can pursue strategic advantage at minimum costs.

This includes an effective risk classification which in turn supports better risk management.

In view of the definition of risk (provided in Chap. 1) as an unfavorable event capable of generating a *negative sign deviation from a given expected situation, such as a smaller gain or a greater loss*, the CEO has the ultimate responsibility to protect the business from such unfavorable events.

Risks, by their own nature, manifest themselves in different ways. They may generate in different areas (the objects of risk, such as corporate functions or processes), involve different stakeholders or external contacts and represent different levels of danger.

Among the risks, that today, worry businesses the most there is, for example, reputational risk a type of transversal risk that may exist in different corporate and governance areas, whose impact is potentially very strong. Like the reputational risk many other unfavorable events, capable of threatening the achievement of corporate objectives, extend beyond the company's individual functions and boundaries, thus tending to become more difficult to foresee and monitor. Moreover, there is a growth of the phenomenon of the interconnection of different risks, which initially manifest themselves inside certain corporate areas but then have their consequences cascading through many other aspects of the internal and external management of the individual business.

Therefore it appears appropriate to consider risk in an integrated fashion, such as the *set of hindrances that threaten the pursuit of the business's objectives*.

For this reason there is the need for a "risk vision" shared by the executive and management areas and a "transversal risk management", directly involving the

A. Borghesi and B. Gaudenzi, *Risk Management*, Perspectives in Business Culture, DOI: 10.1007/978-88-470-2531-8_3, © Springer-Verlag Italia 2013

governance body (entrepreneur/CEO) and drawing from the specialist skills of management in the various corporate areas (Gaudenzi 2006).

Despite this, risks are traditionally broken down into different categories and their management may be tackled from different perspectives.

## 3.2 From the Risk Spectrum to the Four Big Risks

As previously highlighted, risk management should use different tools and approaches, adapted from time to time to the features of the subject of risk, i.e., the corporate processes, sub-systems, and super-systems being analysed. This, for the purpose of properly identifying and managing the threats to the pursuit of objectives. In literature we often find mentioned management tools derived from the world of finance dubbed "highly flexible", i.e., capable of measuring risks of different kinds. We wish to stress, in no uncertain terms, that these tools are definitely very useful, but their use should always go hand in hand with tools of a different kind, for example, process-based measurement methods, linked to performance in terms of efficiency, effectiveness, and profitability.

Taking as reference the possible risk classifications (economic and non-economic, static and dynamic, pure and speculative as described in Chap. 1), here we wish to analyse the current line of thinking on the subject of risk management that can be found in literature and managerial practices.

In order to better interpret this line of thinking, it is worthwhile to recall the representation put forward by Kloman, as early as 1992, of the so-called *risk spectrum*, where the so-called Global Risks and Organizational Risks are identified. That presentation distinguishes *internal risks* from *external risks* to the subject of risk being considered (be it a particular process or the whole business). Such internal and external risks are capable of mutually influencing each other, as in the current concept of "extended governance", and the company may act on such risks either directly (internal risks) or indirectly (external risks) (Fig. 3.1).

The Risk Spectrum has been an essential base for the purpose of defining the organization's risks vis-à-vis the risks of the environments in which it operates and represents a starting point to analyse the far more complex case of a subject of risk that does not coincide with the organization alone, but rather with a system of which it is a part. In this case we may identify three risk levels:

- risks internal to the organization;
- risks typical of the system to which it belongs and therefore partially modifiable and manageable;
- external risks.

An example of a system to which the organization belongs (sub-system) and in turn incorporated in a wider environment (superior system) is the logistics chain (*supply chain*).

Indeed a number of authors have referred risk analysis to factors that are inside and outside the company, linking them to the size of the supply chain. Christopher

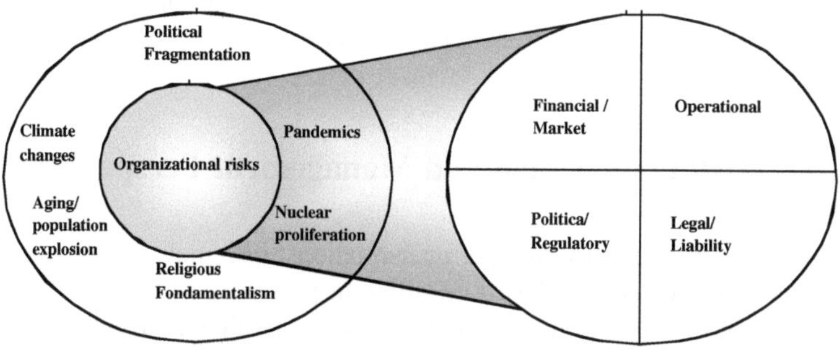


**Fig. 3.1** Kloman's risk spectrum. *Source* modified from (Kloman 1992)

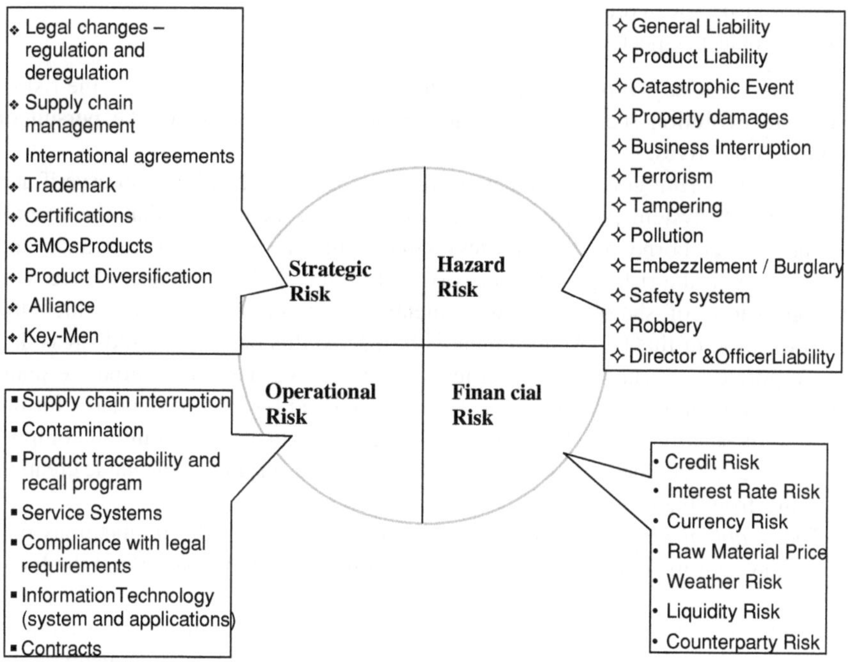


**Fig. 3.2** Four types of risks

(2003) and Svanberg (2004), for example, identify internal and external risk factors, whereas Jüttner et al. (2003) suggest a three tier breakdown:

- external to the entity being analyzed;
- linked to the system of relationships that the entity creates with other entities (businesses with businesses or processes with processes);
- internal to the entity being analysed.

The Risk Spectrum is a common base from which different classifications have generated. Here, we will refer to one which is very well-known, that typically encompasses the four types of risk, and relevant examples (Fig. 3.2).

## 3.3 Four Risk Observation and Management Perspectives

Risks, in their different forms and inter-relationships, may be the subject of observation and management based on different perspectives.

The main risk observation perspectives stem in particular from studies in the economic-corporate and production areas, and may be summarized as:

- strategic perspective;
- corporate governance perspective;
- financial perspective;
- operational perspective.

The *strategic observation* perspective allows us to observe if and how "the risks" linked to evolution scenarios and internal processes may hinder the pursuit of strategic objectives.

In the *corporate governance* perspective, on the other hand, we observe if and how the risk system is such as to guarantee the stakeholders that the overall riskiness level borne by the business falls within a certain risk tolerance and conforms with the risk appetite that is typical of stakeholders, in accordance with the provisions of shareholders' agreements and corporate plans on which the legitimization of the Top Management is based. To this end, we should stress that by Corporate Governance, as specifies hereinafter, we mean the corporate management and compliance system vis-à-vis internal and legislative standards for the purpose of ensuring the achievement of objectives. This stems from the commitment to the stakeholders of ensuring with "reasonable certainty" the value creation resulting from the objectives.

The *financial observation* perspective aims at observing the implications that the risk system may have on the business liquidity, both in the short-and the long-term.

Finally, in the *business perspective*, we observe if and how the risk system may hinder the pursuit of effectiveness and efficiency objectives in managing the processes under observation.

Therefore it emerges that, with a view to detecting the many facets and forms under which they appear, risks should be simultaneously observed from many and different perspectives.

The observation of risk from each of these different perspectives is strictly linked to the adoption of specific management perspectives, from which it stems that the observer (or observers) adopts management tools that are typical of specific areas of responsibility. Therefore, we may envisage the following management perspectives:

- governance management perspective;
- business management perspective;
- financial management perspective.

The governance management perspective tends to embody the management of the risks that were observed from both a strategic and governance point of view. This means managing those risks, seen as both unfavorable events and opportunities, linked to the activity of the governance body committed to ensure compliance with objectives and strategic plans, thus, safeguarding the management integrity and ensuring an overall risk level which is tolerable for the company and its stakeholders.

The business management perspective aims at managing risk in its typical and current form, by managing all its typical traits. Finally, the financial perspective aims at managing the impact that the risk occurrence may have on the components and financial balance of the business.

The distinction between the above observation and management perspectives appears to aim essentially at comprehending the holistic dimension of risk that manifests itself at different levels of corporate life and requires different management approaches.

This perspective has also resulted in the consolidation of a classification of risk categories, over the years, that, however, we do not consider similarly convincing. These categories, for which we will discuss herein the doubts as to their relevance, are:

- strategic and governance risk;
- financial risk;
- business risk.

In general, risks may have strategic, operational, and financial effects and impacts, irrespective of a statically identified risk category. Furthermore, a negative effect resulting from this classification is that it seems to suggest a "combination" between risk categories and those corporate functions that have the jurisdiction for managing them. From this perspective, Top Management would seem to be managing strategic risks, the Finance Department the financial risks and Middle-Management specific activities, whereby *operational* risks losing sight the major existing mutual influences. This would lead to neglecting the transversal dimension of risk, with the ensuing danger of observing each risk from a unilateral perspective.

For example, financial risk is an umbrella term for multiple types of risk associated with negative events related to (for example) credit, liquidity, financial markets.

Financial risks have been defined as "The risk that a company will not have adequate cash flow to meet financial obligations", also described as *movements in exchange rates, commodity prices, interest rates, and stock prices* (Horcher 2005). However, many types of strategic and business risks could have significant financial impacts.

**Table 3.1** Strategic, financial and business perspectives in risk analysis

| *Example of risk* | *Observation perspectives*<br>*How the risk being considered may be seen* | | | *Management perspectives*<br>*Examples of actions* | | |
|---|---|---|---|---|---|---|
| Risk and its description | Strategic perspective | Financial perspective | Business perspective | Strategic Management | Financial Management | Business Management |
| Excess stock at warehouse<br>A stock level exceeding the optimum level (as describes at standard level) entails greater management costs and the risk that the goods being stocked will perish | Warehouse = product lifeline to meet the demands of an unpredictable market | Warehouse = cost in terms of circulating assets and fixed assets | Warehouse = stock linked to logistic-production dynamics | Adjustment of stock level to prevent the risk of missed sales | Adjustment of stock level to optimize liquidity | Adjustment of stock level depending on logistic-production variables |

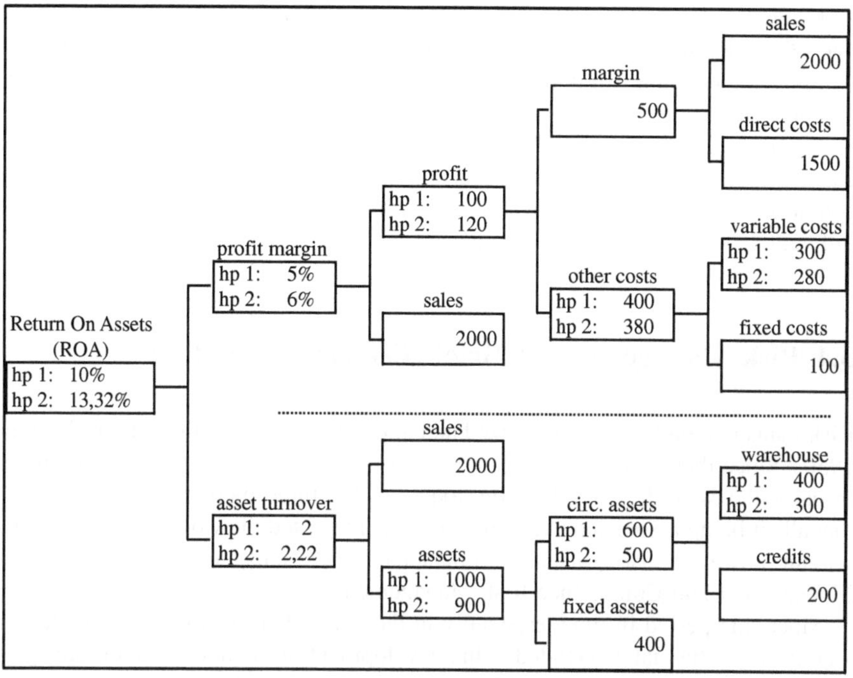


**Fig. 3.3** The Bowersox's model. Source: Adapted from Bowersox et al. 2006

Table 3.1 shows an example referred to the link between the financial perspective and the business perspective: the risk linked to *excess stock* (Waters 2003), of which we briefly describe the versatility from the different observation perspectives. The high level of stock (which may be described as "excessive" if observed from the sole perspective of efficiency and effectiveness of the warehousing process) may, however, be interpreted differently from a risk viewpoint. Indeed it may represent a form of *stock out* (missed sales) risk mitigation, and therefore, a form of risk abatement covering the lack of service to customers. At the same time, however, the management of high stock levels represents a management cost that can hinder the management fluidity and efficiency.

In literature, the link between financial perspective and business perspective, on the very issue of stock management, was analysed by Bowersox, who highlights how the Return on Assets (ROA) varies as a result of the variation of warehousing costs and variable costs which are managed in a logistics context (Bowersox et al. 2006).

This example allows us to highlight how the different perspectives (strategic, financial and business) which embody the typical objectives of the respective functions to which they belong, tend to suggest diverse risk management initiatives, whose reconciliation cannot but occur on the basis of a joint and shared assessment of the different perspectives.

Likewise, the above risk (excess stock at warehouse), albeit representing just one of all possible examples, proves how it cannot be confined to a single risk "class" (for example, strategic, financial or operational risk) because this would misrepresent or diminish its meaning and potential significance.

In our opinion, one of the reasons why we have ended up with such a classification between strategic, financial, and business risks lies in the historical evolution of the risk management process, which at different times has emphasized different aspects of risk and risk management (Fig. 3.3).

## 3.4 Risk Management: A Brief Historical Evolution

Risk management had been theorized and applied in a systematic fashion since the 1950s. Since then, to date Risk Management has undergone significant evolutions, in particular with the consolidation, today, of the three main currents of thought that albeit being associated with a unitary and integrated view of risk management, remain however distinguishable: Financial Risk Management, Business Risk Management and Compliance Risk Management.

Since this period in time, especially in the U.S. where recovery was rapid and significant, industrial growth led to the development of the first tools for managing the "industrial risk", understood in particular as every unfavorable event capable of causing interruptions to production activities, quality defects and damage to production equipment. The risk management applications, which stem mainly from the theories of Total Quality Management and tools such as FMEA, FMECA, Fault Tree, etc., therefore focused on "operational risks" and on the management of business processes.

Previously, however, the role and skills of the risk manager were aimed not so much at preventing risks, through techniques that were typical of the planning and production functions, but rather at managing (in particular insurance transfer) insurable risks, i.e., pure risks, linked especially to the occurrence of incidents that could damage the company's physical and human resources (Dickinson 2004). The center of responsibility was typically the finance function, which took care of *insurance buying* (selection and management of insurance policies). This led to the frequent identification of the risk manager with the *insurance buyer*.

In the 1970s Europe and the United States witnessed the rise of the first positions on the need for an integrated Risk Management approach. Some authors maintained that the risk manager was responsible solely for pure insurable risks, whereas the business risks should be managed by Top Management and the individual functions (Williams et al. 1976).

On the other hand, other authors stressed the importance of a center of responsibility for the management of risk which would be responsible for managing all risks in an integrated and transversal fashion (Greene 1981).

As of the 1980s, as a result of the evolution of competitive and financial markets, new positions on the issue of risk management began consolidating.

Some of the theories already focused on risk management in business processes, have contributed to the development of studies on *crisis management* (see also Chap. 8), analysing not only the aspects of crises stemming from natural events or linked to traditional insurable pure risks, but studying also the ways of restoring and recovering competitiveness, production activities, and image (*contingency planning* and *business continuity management*) in the individual business and also in the networks of business-to-business relationships (Mitroff et al. 2001; Myers 1999; Ogrizek and Guillery 1999). This school may be described today as “Business Risk Management”. In particular, the authors Young and Tippins (2001) define a transversal risk category, the *business risks*, which is identifiable and measurable in seven “risk areas”: physical, social, political, legal, economic, operational, and cognitive. These *business risks* and the relevant risk areas, described by the authors as *environmental sources of risk*, transversally, combine both the global and the organizational risks that are present in the risk spectrum. Noteworthy is also the contribution of such authors when they maintain that the choice of the methods for identifying and measuring risk should depend on the features of such “risk areas”.

Again previously, the financial and insurance-related theories, driven by the changes that occurred on financial and capital markets, agreed on the need of an “extended” view of risk management. To this end “innovative financial and insurance-based instruments were developed”, which (the former) were capable of supporting the risk identification and measurement process in different management areas, thus extending their application scope. This has determined, especially in large and highly structured businesses, the birth of new integrated financial Risk Management approaches.

These two positions have been consolidating over the years and are partly still relevant these days. Indeed there continues to exist a distinction between those who identify risk management through a financial and insurance-based approach and those who, instead, believe that risk management process should be integrated in all corporate processes and functions. This distinction does not concern solely different schools of thought but rather different corporate practices and traditions. Many businesses adopt risk management from a financial and insurance-based perspective, thus neglecting wholly or partially the observation and management of risks that affect processes (*business processes*), thus maintaining a view of the functional risk, managed according to a “silo” approach.

## References


Bowersox DJ, Closs DJ, Cooper MB (2006) Supply chain logistics management, 2nd edn. McGraw Hill, New York

Christopher M (2003) Understanding supply chain risk. Cranfield University, Cranfield

Dickinson G (2004) Enterprise risk management: its origin and conceptual foundation. Geneva Paper Risk Ins 26(3):360–366

Gaudenzi B (2006) Nuovi approcci di gestione dei rischi d'impresa: verso l'integrazione tra imprenditore e management. Sinergie 71:219–242

Greene MR, Serbein ON (1981) Risk management: text and cases. Reston Publishing, New York

Horcher KA (2005) Essentials of financial risk management. Wiley, New York

Jüttner U, Peck H, Christopher M (2003) Supply chain risk management: outlining an agenda for future research. Int J Logistics Res Appl 6(4):197–210

Kloman HF (1992) Rethinking risk management. Geneva Papers, July

Mitroff II, Anagnos G (2001) Managing crises before they happen. Amacom, New York.

Myers KN (1999) Manager's guide to contingency planning for disasters. Wiley, New York

Ogrizek M, Guillery JM (1999) Communicating in crisis. Aldine De Gruyter, New York

Svanberg J (2004) A constructive approach to the interaction between risk and logistics. Department of Design Science, Lund University, Lund, p 29

Waters D (2003) Logistics. An introduction to supply chain management. Palgrave, New York

Williams CA, Heins RM (1976) Risk management & insurance. Mc-Graw Hill, New York

Young PC, Tippins SC (2001) Managing business risk: an organization-wide approach to risk management. Amacom, New York

# Part II
# Risk Assessment: Approaches, Techniques and Good Practices

# Chapter 4
# The Need for an Enterprise-Wide Approach to Risk Management

## 4.1 Enterprise Risk Management

An integrated risk management approach allows for the integration and coordination of strategic entrepreneurial risk management processes through the effective and efficient management of the risks that are typical of business processes, while meeting the performance expectations of the various stakeholders.

The major benefits of an integrated risk management approach are:

- assessing those risks which can threaten a company's competitive edge, protecting and enhancing organizational value (value-based theory);
- supporting the decision-making processes and focusing managers' attention on value creation priorities;
- optimizing the cost of capital and the cost of risk;
- protecting corporate image, reputation, and relationships with stakeholders;
- protection of the company from potential adverse impacts of regulatory issues and formal assessment systems.

Integrated risk management requires capability to move from a silo approach to a systemic approach (system theory, as described in previous chapters).

Integrated Risk Management is known by many names: Business Risk Management, holistic Risk Management, strategic Risk Management, and Enterprise Risk Management.

Putting the name aside for a moment we note that the principles of integrated risk management are clearly stated in ISO 31000. These principles, first published in 2009, are now considered the internationally agreed standard for the definition and implementation of risk management principles.

A major factor to the building of an integrated approach is the Enterprise Risk Management (ERM) framework (2002). This framework, published in 2004 by COSO (Committee of Sponsoring Organizations of the Treadway Commission) has gained increased consideration because it is linked to the requirements of Sarbanes–Oxley for companies listed in the United States.

A. Borghesi and B. Gaudenzi, *Risk Management*, Perspectives in Business Culture,
DOI: 10.1007/978-88-470-2531-8_4, © Springer-Verlag Italia 2013

The term "enterprise" is intended to stress the integrated and holistic nature of the risk management model put forward in this document.

The ERM framework also considers important control and consultation tools for the purpose of meeting both external and internal compliance requirements.

Although the holistic approach provided by the ERM framework is truly valuable, nevertheless we should raise three important shortcomings:

1. The perspective of business processes are included in the class of "operations" that only result in operational risks. Therefore, this approach seems to lack an integrated vision of risk in management activities and a fair consideration of all perspectives. Indeed, risk assessment should be based on the identification, typically by corporate management, of unfavorable events that have both a strategic and operational impact. According to this viewpoint, the entrepreneur, Top Management, and Management should therefore participate in the process of identification of the strategic priorities of the various processes and in the management and control of the latter.
2. Moreover, the ERM framework identifies financial methods as optimum methods for risk assessment, as it considers them suited to being "global", "holistic", and even "strategic", as critically pointed out by Young and Tippins (2001). This would appear to be somewhat limited in scope.
3. Finally, the inter-functional risk assessment would, to a large extent, be referred, according to the ERM framework, to the central coordination role played by an *internal audit*[1]; which is often acknowledged as a possible coordinator of risk management.

Indeed, several surveys and reports released between 2009 and 2010 on risk management, e.g., the Economist Intelligence Unit (www.eiu.com), highlight certain weaknesses of risk management, including less than 50 % of CROs (Chief Risk Officers) are involved in risk identification and analysis; in particular

- Less than 50 % of CROs consider the link between corporate and business risk management as adequate;
- Less than 50 % of enterprises have a risk manager. In fact many organizations have entrusted the risk management function to the internal audit department, the Board or the Chief Financial Officer.

[1] In particular, the International Standards for the Professional Practice of Internal Auditing maintain that the internal auditing should support the enterprise in assessing risks and adopting control measures (*the internal audit activity should help the organization manage risk by identifying and assessing significant exposures to risk and contributing to the improvement of risk management and control systems*).

### 4.1.1 *Internal Auditing and Risk Management: Collaboration, Not Overlap!*

In many cases the internal audit function cooperates with the risk management function.

Companies that do not have an explicit risk management team often utilize the internal audit team as risk management consultants.

This collaboration can work well under certain conditions.

Those conditions highlighted by Knight (2010) are:

- Management remains responsible for risk management. Internal audit should not manage any risks on behalf of management. Whenever internal audit acts to help the management team to set up or to improve risk management processes, its plan of work should include a clear strategy and timeline for migrating the responsibility for these activities to members of the management team[2];
- The nature of internal audit responsibilities should be documented in the audit charter and approved by the Audit Committee. Any work beyond the assurance activities should be recognized as a consulting engagement and the implementation standards related to such engagements should be followed[3];
- Internal audit should provide advice, challenge, and support to management's decision making, as opposed to taking risk management decisions themselves. Internal audit cannot give objective assurance on any part of the risk management framework for which it is responsible. Such assurance should be provided by other suitably qualified parties.

## 4.2 Business Risk Management

The Risk Management process should have as an objective the management of risks that threaten the pursuit of the corporate strategy and objectives. For this reason, the risk management process must include different monitoring and management approaches. Monitoring and management would be integrated to include:

- financial vision;
- business approach;
- integration between strategic and operational approaches.

[2] IIA-UK ERM Position Statement.

[3] IIA Professional Practices Framework and IIA-UK ERM Position Statement.

Business risk does not concern only those industries (e.g. pharmaceutical, heavy industry, building and construction, etc.) whose core business typically requires strict process risk prevention and protection procedures.

Indeed, *business risk* may be described as an unfavorable event resulting from errors or inadequacies which may be linked to corporate processes, systems, human resources, and external events.

We note that a similar description was put forward in the banking sector for the concept of operational risk (Basel Committee on Banking Supervision 2004). As indicated above this concept is not complete due to some scope limitations.

The business risk may therefore be linked with further risk areas, often considered separate but at the same time prone to being associated with the concept of business risk (Christopher and Gaudenzi 2009):

- risks associated with human resources;
- risks associated with IT systems;
- risks associated with errors or non-compliance by internal processes;
- risks associated with errors or non-compliance by external processes, vis-à-vis other enterprises linked to one another by business relationships;
- risks associated with business interruption.

Starting from this business context, as we will see in greater detail in the subsequent chapters, risk management applies to each of these business areas:

- internal area: management of risks associated with human resources, safety and health, intellectual capital, fraud and corruption events;
- networking area: management of risks associated with outsourcing and supply chain management;
- integration area: management of risks associated with the environment, products and markets, both commercial and financial;
- transparency area: management of compliance risks vis-à-vis binding legislation;
- corporate ethics area: management of reputational risks.

Many of these business risks have both strategic and operational value, and for this reason there will be a separation between business risk and operational risk.

Research by CERM View (Norland Managed Services Customers) estimated that 90 % of high impact risks, associated with management rather than environmental factors, may be linked to human or process errors. In these cases, such risks, in view of the impact of their consequences, have a definite strategic value.

We should always remember that "one model does not fit all companies" (Barton et al. 2002). Differences are due to the type of business and competition models employed by the organization, the background of top management and, last but not least, the size of the enterprise.

Typically, risk is most formally managed in large enterprises, which are equipped with complex and articulated organizational structures. Small enterprises, on the other hand, at times do not implement a risk management approach at all, or, conversely, centralize in the entrepreneur a risk cross-management which, however, is neither formalized nor planned.

**Fig. 4.1** Risk management areas

## 4.3 Risk Management in the Organizational Structure

The levels at which risk management should be developed are the following (Holfmann 2010, Pidgeon et al. 1992).

- *Governance Area*
  - governance and compliance initiatives are embedded, coordinated, and more efficiently managed.
- *Strategic Area*
  - reaching a better level of control reducing unacceptable performance variability;
  - all significant risks that can threaten the achievement of business objectives and strategies are identified and properly addressed in a timely manner;
  - strategic and Business Plans are more robust and in line with Organization's risk appetite;
  - resources are allocated based on risk-return analysis;
- *Management Area*
  - silo approach is broken, risk culture and awareness are spread and cascaded across, up and down the organization;
  - existing risk management practices are harmonized, aligned, and improved across the organization.
- *Organizational Area*
  - all significant risks have responsible owners and are reported at the appropriate executive level
  - risk Management is more transparent and cross divisional.

In summary, Figs. 4.1 and 4.2 combines the different risk management approaches and some of the central managerial areas that will be discussed in the following chapters.

At the different organizational levels, risk management responsibilities can be defined as follows:

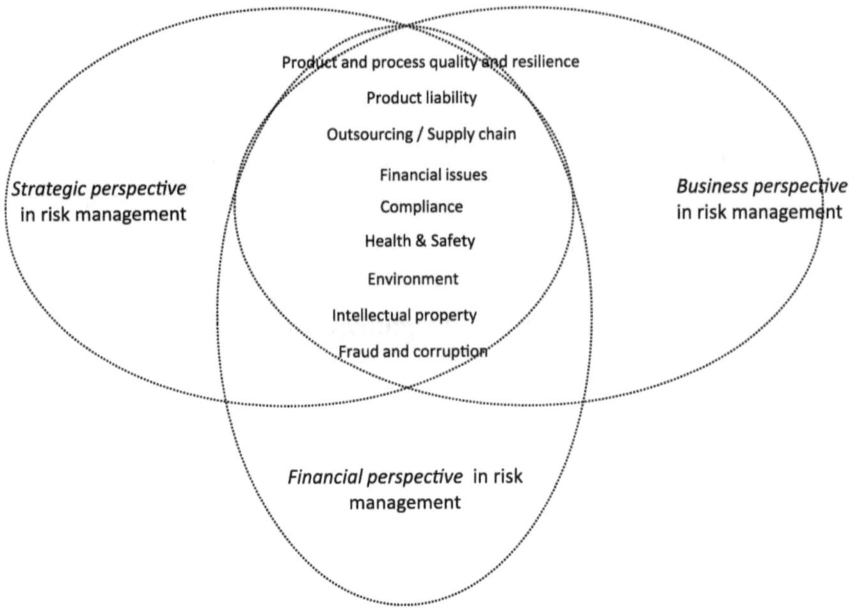


**Fig. 4.2** Strategic, financial, and business perspectives in risk management

- CEO/Board: Determine strategic approach to governance and risk.
- Hence, the CEO establishes how to build the risk management and how to prioritize the most significant risks
- Business Unit Manager: build risk awareness culture within the unit and agree to risk management performance targets.
  - ensure implementation of risk improvement recommendations.
  - identify and report changed circumstances/risks.
- RM responsibilities for individual employees: understand, accept, and implement RM processes:
  - report inefficient, unnecessary, or unworkable controls;
  - report loss events and near-miss incidents;
  - co-operate with management on incident investigations.
- RM responsibilities for the risk manager:
  - develop the risk management policy and keep it up-to-date;
  - document the internal risk policies and structures;
  - coordinate the risk management (and internal control) activities;
  - compile risk information and prepare reports for the Board.

**Table 4.1** The three mainstays of an integrated risk management

| Specialization and integration in the various functions | Integrated management of major "unfavorable events" | Priority to so-called critical risks |
| --- | --- | --- |
| Adopting suitable risk assessment tools in each corporate area;<br>Sharing risk assessment and decisions in an inter-functional team;<br>Sharing responsibilities among the Board, the risk manager, and company contacts | Monitoring risks from a strategic, financial, and business perspective (for each type of risk);<br>Managing risks (assessment, control and monitoring) for the purpose of mitigating its overall impact on the enterprise. | Setting out, upstream, management priorities;<br>Identifying, among all the risks being monitored, the critical risks and analyzing their correlations in order to fully assess their impact;<br>Making decisions consistently with strategic priorities |

- RM responsibilities for specialist risk management functions:
  - assist the company in establishing specialist risk policies;
  - develop specialist contingency and recovery plans;
  - keep up-to-date with developments in the specialist area;
  - support investigations of incidents and near misses.
- RM responsibilities for internal audit manager:
  - develop a risk-based internal audit program;
  - audit the risk processes across the organization;
  - receive and provide assurance on risk management;
  - report on the efficiency and effectiveness of internal controls.

The strategic, financial, and business management approaches should always coexist and integrate with one another. This is due to the fact that many risks may have, at the same time, financial and/or strategic and/or operational implications, as outlined in the previous chapter (see Fig. 4.2).

It is therefore necessary to implement a risk management process that allows a cross-analysis of risks, and identification of the different nuances, influences, and correlations.

For this purpose the three mainstays of an integrated risk management are highlighted in Table 4.1.

In order to make the three mainstays truly effective, it is necessary that:

- upstream, top management is committed to the implementation of an integrated risk management process which aims to protect the enterprise from unfavorable events. For this reason, it is similarly necessary that the Company management set out priorities, in light of which the priorities for risk treatment choices are set out;
- during the process, the risk management role is essential, the in-depth knowledge of the operational activities and the processes being monitored directly facilitate implementation.

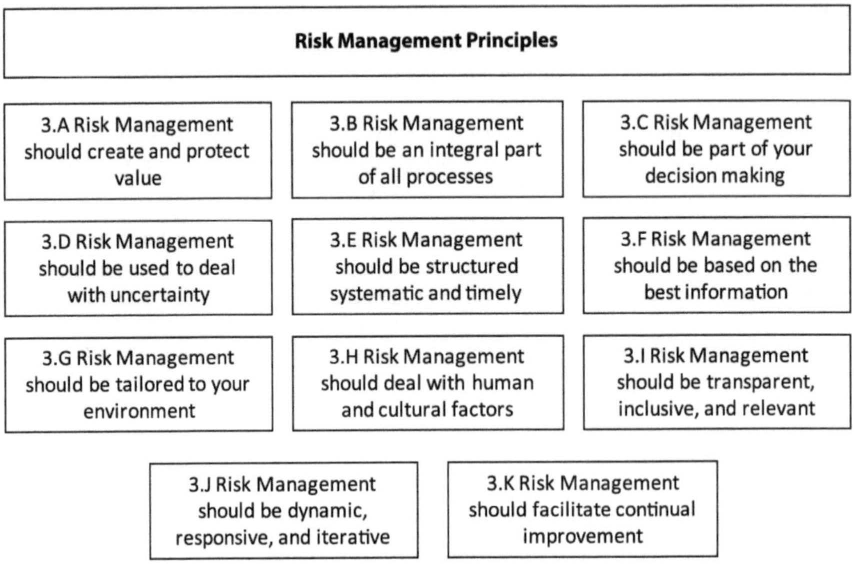


**Fig. 4.3** Risk management principles

Therefore, an integrated approach allows the organization to:

- monitor the interdependency relationships among several unfavorable events that may result in cascading consequences capable of involving several corporate areas;
- improve transparency in the strategic decision-making stages;
- implement a more selective process for transferring risk to third parties, with a resulting reduction in risk treatment costs.

## 4.4 ISO 31000 (2009)

As mentioned previously the ISO 31000 (2009) is an international standard which provides a structured approach to risk management. ISO also produced Guide 73 "Risk management—Vocabulary—Guidelines for use in the standards". The establishment of a common risk management language is essential to the successful sharing of information, establishment of metrics, and communicating results.

The ISO 31000:2009 sets out the principles (Fig. 4.3), a framework (Fig. 4.4) and a risk management process (Fig. 4.5) that are applicable to almost any type of organization. It highlights that a principle-based risk management approach must be tailored to each organization, to specific needs, structure, and purpose of the organization.

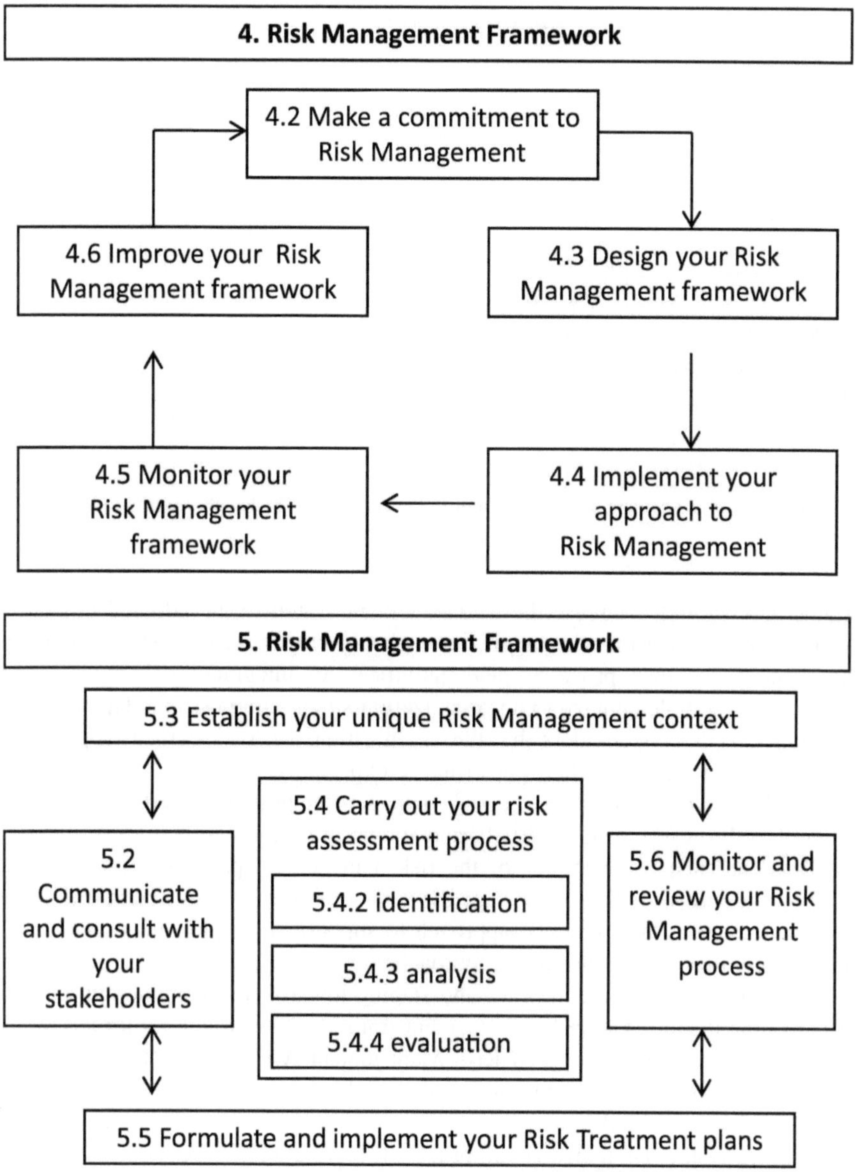


**Fig. 4.4** Risk management framework and process. *Source* adapted from Knight 2010

The previously mentioned 11 principles set the stage for an organization to protect the value creation mechanisms by managing risks effectively and efficiently (Fig. 4.3).

It almost goes without saying that a risk management process should be consistent with the framework that the organization defines. A risk management

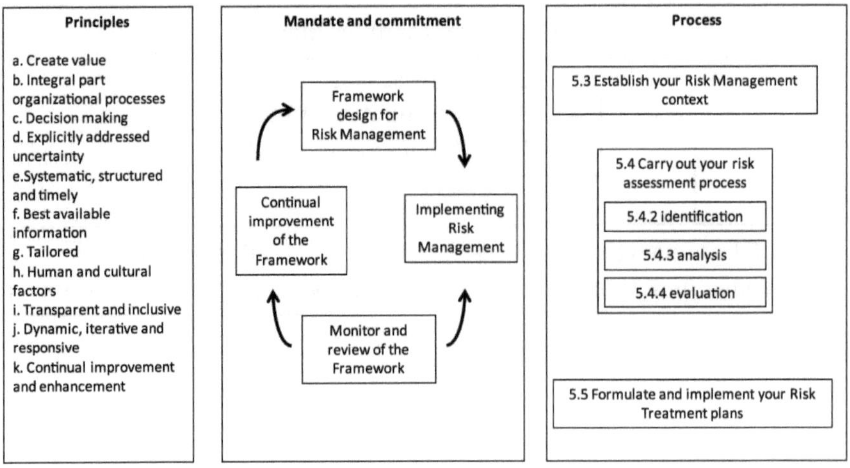


**Fig. 4.5** Risk management principles-framework and process in Knight. *Source* adapted from Knight 2010

framework should not prescribe a management system to be adopted but rather emphasizes the fact that the organization should customize the risk management approach to its own processes and activities. An integrated risk management approach is complementary to an organization's value proposition. This provides assurance to the stakeholders that the organization risk management approach is aligned and in tune with their performance expectations.

A different view of integrated risk management principles and framework is offered by Professor Knight (2010), and shown in Fig. 4.5.

These are just two versions of the risk management process, principles, and framework and while they may stage the steps in a somewhat different order they follow a common best practice approach to support the implementation of complete integrated risk management approach.

This concept of different views and staging towards a systematic approach to establishing a solid-state risk management framework is further confirmed by the views of many of the European Risk Management Associations (FERMA, AIRMIC, BELRIM) as well as International Risk Management Associations such as IFRIMA, RIMS, ARIMA, and GARP.

In all cases the risk management process is highlighted for being consistent and in coordination with the corporate governance framework, its direction, executive action, supervision, and accountability stages (Boyd 1997).

These international perspectives on the risk management principles, framework, and processes are increasing their focus on all stakeholders, as they are crucial both for risk management framework and for corporate governance framework.

ISO 31000 (2009) 5.2 Stakeholders Identification

Communication and consultation with stakeholders is important as they make judgments about risk based on their perceptions of risk. These perceptions can vary due to differences in values, needs, assumptions, concepts, and concerns of stakeholders. As their views can have a significant impact on the decisions made, the stakeholders' perceptions should be identified, recorded, and taken into account in the decision-making process.

Communication and consultation should facilitate truthful, relevant, accurate, and understandable exchanges of information, taking into account confidential and personal integrity aspects. Source: http://www.iso.org

Stakeholders are defined as (ISO 31000, 2009; Knight 2010):

- customers;
- decision-makers;
- individuals inside the organization, such as employees, management;
- individuals or groups who are interested in issues related to the proposal;
- individuals who are, or perceive themselves to be, directly affected by a decision or activity;
- non-government organizations such as environment groups and public interest groups;
- partners in the decision, such as financial institutions and insurance agencies;
- government officials (at all government levels) who may have an electoral or portfolio interest;
- regulators and other government organizations that have authority over activities; senior management, contractors, and volunteers;
- suppliers and service providers;
- the media, who are likely stakeholders as well as channels of information to other stakeholders;
- union and/or other employee representative groups.

## References

Barton TL, Shenkir WG, Walker PL (2002) Making enterprise risk management pay off. Financial Times Prentice Hall, London

Basel Committee on Banking Supervision, International Convergence of Capital Measurement and Capital Standards: a revised framework, 2004

Boyd J (1997) Risk management's role in corporate governance. Corp Risk 4:8

Christopher M, Gaudenzi B (2009) Exploiting knowledge through reputation management. Ind Mark Manage 38:131–137

Committee of Sponsoring Organizations of the Treadway Commission (COSO) (2002–2004) Internal control-integrated Framework (ICIF). www.erm.coso.org
Holfmann E (2010) Linking corporate strategy and supply chain management. Int J Phys Distrib Logist Manage 40(4):256–276
Knight KW (2010) Risk Management. A journey.. not a destination, Standards Australia/ Standards New Zeland Joint Thecnical Committee. http://mgubs.ru/images/Image/A%20 Journey%20Not%20A%20Destination.pdf.pdf
Pidgeon N, Hood C, Jones D, Turner B, (1992) Risk perception. Iin: Risk: analysis, perception and management. The Royal Society, London
Young PC, Tippins SC (2001) Managing business risk: an organization-wide approach to risk management. AMACOM

# Chapter 5
# Risk Identification

## 5.1 What is Risk Identification?

Risk identification is a distinct activity part of the risk assessment process. As stated in the ISO 31.000/2009, risk assessment consists of risk identification, analysis, and evaluation of all areas across the entire organization.

Looking at this definition in more detail we can say that risk assessment and hence risk identification should be considered a dual track process.

The first track involves each risk area/process and the fact that each area/process has a risk owner, who is responsible for ensuring that those risks are effectively assessed and formally addressed. This would also include the continuous monitoring of the risk assessment processes and procedures implemented. The goal is to prioritize risks which are more critical, in order to support management in responding appropriately (Barton et al. 2002).

The second track involves the Board in a role of validation and sign off on the prioritization of the risks that impact value creation and shareholder value. In this way risk assessment process forms an integral part of the strategic and corporate planning process (COSO 2002–2004).

Building from these two tracks we can then look more specifically at the role of risk identification in the Integrated Risk Management approach.

**ISO 31000 (2009). 5.4.2. Risk Identification**
The aim of this step is to generate a comprehensive list of risks based on those events that might create, enhance, prevent, degrade, accelerate, or delay the achievement of objectives. It is important to identify the risks associated with not pursuing an opportunity. Comprehensive identification is critical, because a risk that is not identified at this stage will not be included in further analysis.

A. Borghesi and B. Gaudenzi, *Risk Management*, Perspectives in Business Culture,
DOI: 10.1007/978-88-470-2531-8_5, © Springer-Verlag Italia 2013

As the *Risk Management Standard Airmic, Alarm, IRM (2002)* stated: "Risk identification sets out to identify an organization's exposure to uncertainty. It should be approached in a methodical way to ensure that all significant activities and all the risks flowing from these activities are defined."

Risk identification may be broken down into the following stages (Hall 2008, Franco-Santos et al. 2007):

1. identification of the unfavorable event: in other words, this means looking for critical risk areas inside the enterprise and identifying potential unfavorable events, i.e. events capable of resulting in losses;
2. analysis of the hazards associated with the event: this means looking for the causes or sources that may give rise to the event. Through the utilization of available standard risk classifications based on causes, we may distinguish between natural events hazards (e.g. hail, lightening, earthquakes, etc.), man-made events (explosions, chemical reactions, etc.), and, finally, human activities (traffic accidents, assessment mistakes, etc.);
3. analysis of related contingencies: in other words, this means identifying the conditions that create or increase the likelihood of an event occurring. This analysis should focus on the contingencies in their various physical, moral, and psychological configurations;
4. identification of the types of effects stemming from the event: this latter logical analysis does not focus solely on measuring the effects (which is the objective of the second stage of the overall risk management process) but rather on the search for the type of potential damage to the enterprise.

The scope of risk identification is to build a template for recording appropriate information about each risk.

Table 5.1 shows the range of information that may need to be recorded in order to build a valid repository for adequate risk assessment (AIRMIC, ALARM, IRM).

Specifically risk identification techniques are designed to provide the organization with the capability to identify potential unfavorable events through the study of business operations.

Possible methods of identifying risks are:

1. organizational charts;
2. flow charts;
3. vulnerability analysis, matrix of interdependencies;
4. checklists;
5. event chain diagrams, decision trees.

Moreover:

6. methods based on intra- and inter-company data exchange: brainstorming, interview/focus group discussions; surveys, questionnaires;
7. strengths, weaknesses, opportunities, and threats (SWOT) analysis.

A more detailed analysis of some of these tools reveal their real utility and in some cases complexity of application.

**Table 5.1** Detailed risk description

| Risk name | Unique identifier or risk index |
|---|---|
| Risk scope | Risk scope and details of possible events, including description of the events, their size, type, and number |
| Risk nature | Risk classification, timescale of potential impact and description as hazard, opportunity, or uncertainty<br>Determination if the impact is strategic, operational, and/or financial? |
| Stakeholders | Stakeholders, both internal and external, and their expectations |
| Risk analysis | Probability and magnitude. Which analysis method is involved (qualitative–quantitative?) |
| Loss experience | Previous incidents and prior loss experience of events related<br>to the risk |
| Risk tolerance, appetite or attitude | Loss potential and anticipated financial impact of the risk<br>Target for risk control and desired level of performance<br>Risk attitude, appetite, tolerance, or limits for the risk |
| Risk response, treatment, and controls | Existing control mechanisms and activities<br>Level of confidence in existing controls<br>Procedures for monitoring and review of risk performance |
| Potential for risk improvement | Potential for cost-effective risk improvement or modification<br>Recommendations and deadlines for implementation<br>Responsibility for implementing any improvements |
| Strategy and policy developments | Responsibility for developing strategy related to the risk<br>Responsibility for auditing compliance with controls |

### *5.1.1 Organizational Charts*

Risk management has been for long time characterized by a "silo approach", where risk owners were dealing with specific risks and risk areas.

The alignment and integration among functions, in order to share valuable risk expertise, can represent an effective way for managing risks more effectively.

Furthermore gaps and overlaps in managing risks across the organization can be addressed and in many cases reduced by the Chief Risk Officer function.

The analysis of the organizational charts may therefore be a useful source of information for the purpose of understanding:

- the degree of centralization or decentralization of the risk management and the CFO's (Chief Financial Officer) functions;
- the degree of decision-making autonomy at various levels;
- the interactions and interrelations between the various functional areas of the organization.

For example, the organizational analysis of the sales function may highlight the company's preference for a particular product (or group of products), a particular customer (or group of customers), or a particular geographical market area. This

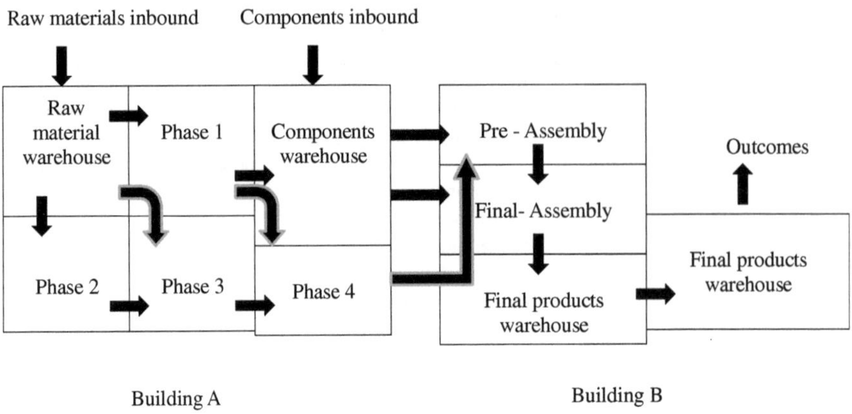


**Fig. 5.1** Simple flow charts

may allow us to identify potential vulnerability situations: a manufacturing defect may be lethal for an enterprise that depends to an excessive extent on a single product; a simple fire affecting a major customer or supplier may result in a serious competitive damage; a natural disaster (earthquake, flood) or socio-political unrest in a particular location may create severe business interruptions along the supply chain.

### *5.1.2 Flow Charts*

Flow charts may be:

- general, if they consider the entire production process for goods or services;
- specific, if they refer to individual departments or divisions.

Moreover, they may be either simple (if they outline only the flow of materials, records, or persons) or weighted (where the flow undergoes a physical or economic measurement).

Flow charts, if properly developed, may provide useful indications as to the critical junctures in a process or supply chain to be analyzed in depth as regards potential hazards or contingencies. A sample of a general and simple flow chart for a production process is shown in Fig. 5.1.

The main drawback of simple flow charts is that they do not provide any information on the degree of enterprise dependency on external economies (suppliers, customers, and so on) and on the relative importance of the various stages of the production process. This may be remedied by developing weighted flow charts. Where possible, it is advisable that the flow measurement is expressed in monetary terms by allocating each processing stage its share of value added. A sample of this type of chart is shown in Fig. 5.2.

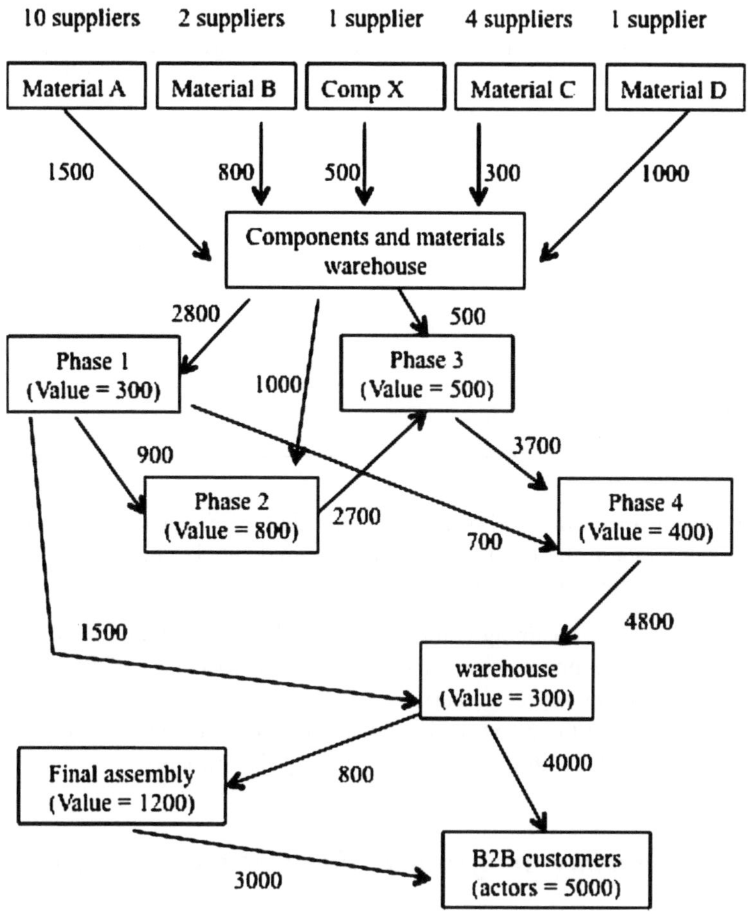


**Fig. 5.2** Weighted flow charts

This chart provides the reader a more accurate picture of the potential impacts of each phase of the process and the risks represented at each step in the process.

In this example the first consideration is that, from the suppliers' standpoint, two components are supplied by a single supplier, thus creating a potential dependency risk (to be assessed based on the value and complexity of the product).

Another worthwhile observation is that almost all of the raw materials and components flow through a single centralized warehouse. It may also be observed that the most important part of production undergoes processing (if we follow the product flows indicated by arrows) and that it transits through a single warehouse. We can also note how the products meant for B2B customers are mostly independent from the final assembly.

**Table 5.2** Exposure table

| | Fire | Theft | Liability | Sabotage | Breakdown | Strike | Illness | Economic trends | Market trends |
|---|---|---|---|---|---|---|---|---|---|
| Buildings | | | | | | | | | |
| Equipment | | | | | | | | | |
| Vehicles | | | | | | | | | |
| Finished products | | | | | | | | | |
| Components | | | | | | | | | |
| Semi-processed products | | | | | | | | | |
| Warehouses | | | | | | | | | |
| IT systems | | | | | | | | | |
| Human resources | | | | | | | | | |
| Records | | | | | | | | | |

Further considerations will be possible after that the risk manager has identified the critical points of the plant under a business and supply chain interruption risk profile. Thus we may be able to assess:

1. the possibility of obtaining components X and D from other sources;
2. whether such components are included or otherwise part of the production supplied to major key customers;
3. the possibility, in the event of significant damage to the warehouse, of directly storing the products in the specific processing departments.

### *5.1.3 Vulnerability Analysis and Matrix of Interdependencies*

The vulnerability analysis may be conducted starting from a double entry table where the main corporate assets (both tangible and intangible) as well as the potential hazards and vulnerability are included.

At each line or column crossing, the risk manager will need to make an assessment as to the existence or otherwise of the risk being considered.

More in detail, the table (an example of which is shown in Table 5.2) allows for representing two types of information:

1. horizontally it provides an immediate highlighting of the assets or group of corporate assets more exposed to risks;
2. vertically it provides a quick identification of the risks recurring with greater frequency.

In the case under examination, we may observe how the assets mostly threatened are buildings and how the most recurring risk is the risk of fire.

A more sophisticated tool for identifying the vulnerability areas inside the enterprise is the matrix for analysis of the interrelations between the various parts of the production process. This analysis allows us to determine the contribution by each of these parts to the enterprise's final economic result.

This information, in turn, is crucial for the purpose of identifying the risks along the production process path and the impacts they may have on the enterprise, in particular in terms of business and supply chain interruption.

The vulnerability analysis may be conducted by analyzing and describing the various types of vulnerability. For example:

- human vulnerability—from individuals or organizations, illness, death, etc.;
- operational vulnerability—from disruption to supplies and operations, loss of access to essential assets, failures in distribution, etc.;
- reputational—from loss of business partner or employee confidence, or damage vulnerability to reputation in the market;
- procedural vulnerability—from failures of accountability, internal systems and controls, organization, fraud, etc.;
- project vulnerability—risks of cost over-runs, jobs taking too long, of insufficient product or service quality, etc.;
- financial vulnerability—from business failure, stock market, interest rates, unemployment, etc.;
- technical vulnerability—from advances in technology, technical failure, etc.;
- natural vulnerability—threats from weather, other natural disasters, accident, disease, etc.;
- political vulnerability—from changes in tax regimes, public opinion, government policy, foreign influence, etc.

### 5.1.4 Checklists

The risk identification process may be significantly rationalized if the identification of risk situations is planned by putting in place standardized monitoring procedures for corporate assets and operations.[1]

The formalization of such procedures generates the so-called checklists that have the purpose of guiding the manager toward an informed and sequential search for risk exposures.

The origin of these lists may be:

[1] See the Appendix to the end of Part 2.

- external: typically these may be developed by insurers, reinsurers, risk management consultants, insurance brokers and consultants, and management experts;
- internal: these are managed by multiple functions within the company.

The criteria used to arrive at the development of checklists may be different depending on the underlying basis:

- *Resource categories* In this case, the starting point will be the listing of the various types of assets (buildings, plant and equipment, materials, enterprise's own products or third-party products falling or otherwise under the enterprise's liability). Each type will then entail a set of queries aimed at highlighting the existing threats and their consequences.
- *Consequence categories* In this case, there will be a listing of the potential unfavorable situations for the enterprise, such as business losses or damage, revenue losses, liability losses, business interruption, and so forth. For each type of consequences, an appropriate questionnaire will help identify the resources involved and existing threats.
- *Threat categories* With possible types of threats (natural forces, human error, willful damage, natural wear, and tear) as a starting point, this checklist will help identify the threatened resources and relevant consequences.
- *Corporate operations categories* In this case, the risk identification planning follows a breakdown of the corporate business into more or less detailed areas (for instance, HR, Procurement, Production, Distribution, Supply Chain, Finance, IT, Legal Office) and the search, in each of these areas, for exposed resources, threats, and consequences through a set of queries.

At a general level, the use of experience, especially statistical data relating to past events, represents a database for both risk identification and risk measurement. This of course, if the event and as many variables as possible that led to its occurrence were recorded.

Nowadays, enterprises process and store checklists for the purpose of performance measurement, compliance and risk management.

In the past, these procedures were widespread within organizations for the purpose of tracking workplace injuries and other events that caused personal damage to third parties, mapping the events covered by insurance policies and finally identifying events that, albeit not falling in the situations described above, had caused significant damage.

Presently, enterprises are increasingly required (due to compliance obligations) and feel the need to methodically map risks of a different nature within the various corporate processes to manage and monitor said risks.

An example of an adaptable and popular (this is also available on line!) risk management checklist is provided by Craig Borysowich (2008) and is discussed in the appendix. This simple checklist is divided into three sections (customer risks, production risks, delivery risks) and describes potential risk sources and ideas for risk reduction. Every company should obviously identify its own checklist, on the basis of its business, competitive environment, and process characteristics. A practical and general example may be a useful starting-point.

In a broader perspective, many other decision-making tools could be adapted to the scope of risk assessment. The goal is to support the management in avoiding poor decisions.

Therefore decision-making skills influence an effective use of risk-assessment techniques. A good decision-making process assures the following capabilities:

- evaluation of risks associated with each alternative before making a decision;
- a well-defined process to analyze risks;
- selection of the proper decision makers (in and outside the company) in risk management decisions;
- running the process in the right time;
- dedication of time and resources to communicate the output of the identification processes;
- monitoring effectiveness and consequences of decisions;
- prioritization (which objective is most important?);
- addressing the limit of personal own experience and instinctive decisions.[2]

### 5.1.5 Event Chain Diagrams and Decision Trees

Event chain diagrams support the uncertainty modeling and schedule network analysis technique that is focused on identifying and managing negative events that affect process schedules. Event chain methodology is an evolution of critical path analysis.

Decision Trees are effective tools for selecting proper courses of action among different alternatives. They provide a highly effective structure which represent different options investigating the possible risks and consequences which may result from choosing those options. Decision Trees also provide a balanced picture of risks and rewards associated with each possible course of action.

We have repeatedly observed how each of the techniques described above cannot completely guarantee the identification of all the hazards and unfavorable events that potentially threaten the enterprise.

Therefore it is the skills of the person called upon to identify the risks to choose the most appropriate mix of techniques they increase the likelihood of success. They must have regard to the nature and specificity of the business carried out and the costs to be incurred to make such techniques operational.

We would recommend as a valid and valuable approach the utilization, as a first action, the identification of critical risk areas, for instance through the matrix

---

[2] Some of these points were taken from www.mindtools.com "How Good Is Your Decision-Making?".

of interdependencies, and then investigate individual risks through external checklists.

## References

AIRMIC, ALARM, IRM, A structured approach to Enterprise Risk Management (ERM) and the requirements of ISO 31000. www.airmic.com

Committee of Sponsoring Organizations of the Treadway Commission (COSO) (2002–2004) Internal control-integrated Framework (ICIF). www.erm.coso.org

Barton TL, Shenkir WG, Walker PL (2002) Making enterprise risk management pay off. Financial Times Prentice Hall, London

Hall M (2008) The effect of comprehensive performance measurement systems on role clarity, psychological empowerment and managerial performance. Acc Organ Soc 33:141–163

Franco-Santos M, Kennerley M, Micheli P, Martinez V, Mason S, Marr B, Gray D, Neely A (2007) Towards a definition of a business performance measurement system. Int J Oper Prod Manag 27(8):784–801

# Chapter 6
# Risk Analysis

Most organizations are aware that risks do not appear on a linear basis and for this reason risk cannot be identified and measured in this way. Assessing and understanding the interrelation of risk and their associated correlated impact is the real challenge. These complex relationships require a different set of tools. Through the use of tools to simulate multiple risk scenarios and correlating risk interdependencies the organization can begin to build an effective map of their risk landscape. The goal is to understand the cumulative impact of risks on performance and value in order to select the appropriate mix between risk retention and risk treatments.

Risk analysis supports managers in understanding the negative impacts of adverse events (in terms of costs or underperformance) and likelihood of negative consequences.

**ISO 31000 (2009). 5.4.3 Risk analysis**
Risk analysis involves developing an understanding of risk and impacts both positive and negative. Risk analysis provides input for risk evaluation and decisions on the most appropriate risk treatment strategies and methods. Risk analysis can also provide input for making decisions where the options involve different types and levels of risk assumption, mitigation, reduction, and avoidance.

Risk is characterized by two basic features:

- the severity of the possible adverse consequences;
- the likelihood (probability) of occurrence of each consequence.

The risk level is defined by the measurement of severity and likelihood.

A. Borghesi and B. Gaudenzi, *Risk Management*, Perspectives in Business Culture,
DOI: 10.1007/978-88-470-2531-8_6, © Springer-Verlag Italia 2013

## 6.1 Qualitative or Quantitative Analysis?

In order to measure risk it is possible to use quantitative and qualitative analysis.

Qualitative analysis is preferable where the level of risk is relatively low, and therefore obtaining the data necessary for data-driven analysis could be too costly.

Moreover, qualitative analysis is recommended when ample information about risks is shared by many persons from different functions, where there is a variety of risk perceptions and backgrounds.

For those situations that fall between qualitative and quantitative risk analysis there is a method that is called semi-quantitative analysis. Semi-quantitative analysis is characterized by the involvement of both quantitative tools and qualitative approaches. It is often identified as the best trade-off between subjective perceptions and rigorous, objective techniques, which provide a good description of likelihood and consequences, calculating the risk level with appropriate data and statistical information.

Typically, the level of accuracy can only be considered generally accurate when semi-quantitative analysis is involved but there are tools that can increase the level of confidence in accuracy some of which are outlined in this chapter.

Quantitative approaches are suitable in the event that likelihood and consequences can be quantified, for example using significant statistical databases. Often one is faced with a lack of sufficient data to apply this technique with a high level of confidence.

In all the cases, the goal of risk analysis is to provide a ranking of inherent and residual risks, and to prioritize and select the "proper" risk treatment actions based on available information and data.

## 6.2 Introduction to Basic Statistical Tools

Likelihood functions play a key role in statistical inference, especially methods of estimating acceptable levels of risk from a set of statistics.

The likelihood of a set of measure values given some observed outcomes is equal to the probability of those observed outcomes given those measure values.

"Likelihood" is often a synonym for "probability" but in statistical use, a clear technical distinction is made.

For example:

One may ask "If I were to flip a fair coin 100 times, what is the probability of it landing heads-up every time?" or "Given that I have flipped a coin 100 times and it has landed heads-up 100 times, what is the likelihood that the coin is fair?" but it would be improper to switch "likelihood" and "probability" in the two sentences (Pawitan 2001).

If a probability distribution depends on a value, one may on one hand consider—for a given value—the probability (density) of the different outcomes,

**Table 6.1** Discrete probability distribution

| No. of failures | Probability |
|---|---|
| 0 | 0.2 |
| 1 | 0.1 |
| 2 | 0.3 |
| 3 | 0.4 |

and on the other hand consider—for a given outcome—the probability (density) this outcome has occurred for different values. The first approach interprets the probability distribution as a function of the outcome, given a fixed value, while the second interprets it as a function of the value, given a fixed outcome. In the latter case the function is called the "likelihood function" of the value, and indicates how likely a value is in light of the observed outcome.

For the definition of the likelihood function, we should distinguish between discrete and continuous probability distributions.

### *6.2.1 Discrete Probability Distribution*

X is a random variable with a discrete probability distribution p depending on a value $\theta$. Then the function

$$L(\theta|x) = p_\theta(x) = P_\theta(X = x),$$

is considered as a function of $\theta$, is called the likelihood function (of $\theta$, given the outcome $x$ of $X$). Sometimes the probability on the value $x$ of $X$ for the value $\theta$ is written as $P(X = x \mid \theta)$, but should not be considered as a conditional probability.

### *6.2.2 Continuous Probability Distribution*

$X$ is a random variable with a continuous probability distribution with density function f depending on a value $\theta$. Then the function

$$L(\theta|x) = f_\theta(x),$$

considered as a function of $\theta$, is called the likelihood function (of $\theta$, given the outcome $x$ of $X$). Sometimes the density function for the value $x$ of $X$ for the value $\theta$ is written as $f(x \mid \theta)$, but should not be considered as a conditional probability density.

The actual value of a likelihood function bears no meaning. Its use lies in comparing one value with another. E.g., one value may be more likely than another, given the outcome of the sample. Or a specific value will be most likely: the maximum likelihood estimate. Comparison may also be performed in considering the quotient of two likelihood values (Table 6.1, Fig. 6.1).

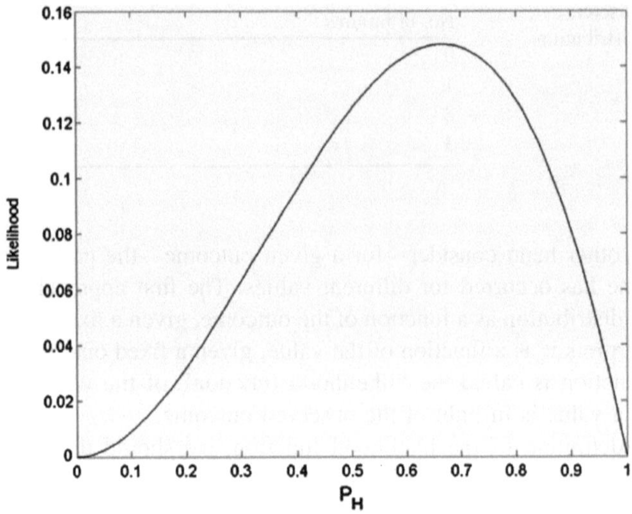


**Fig. 6.1** Continuous probability distribution

The risk analysis should run on specific assets, like an individual tangible asset (such as a machine or a building) or intangible asset (such as lost earnings, goodwill, reputation, etc.), or an individual person (such as an employee). However, it could also run on a complex of assets (like a company or a department) or persons (all personnel), or even an entire manufacturing facility (intended as the complex of tangible assets and persons).

The identification of the assets is a major issue because it is also in relation to such assets that we may collect the historical data based on which we will then develop the probable frequency and severity distribution.

An asset may be analyzed in relation to the individual risks, either separately or by groups of assets. Thus, it is possible to analyze the exposure of an individual asset to the risk of fire, vandalism, business interruption, etc.

For example, a motor vehicle may be exposed to the risk of third-party liability, whereas it could be part of a wider asset such as the manufacturing facility, relating to the risk of fire, should the vehicle's garaging location be located inside such a facility.

A final, but just as important a consideration, concerns the possibility of measuring risks for either single assets or groups of assets.

This possibility plays a major role in the reliability assessment that may refer to past experiences in order to foresee future ones, as the direct link between the number of findings and the frequency of their likely occurrence is a known fact.

This is a crucial asset classification and grouping issue, which needs to be solved by having special regard to the homogeneity and independence of such assets.

**Table 6.2** Probability and gravity

| Frequency | Probability |
|---|---|
| 0 | 0.10 |
| 1 | 0.60 |
| 2 | 0.25 |
| 3 | 0.05 |
| total | 1.00 |

## 6.3 Probable Maximum Loss and Annual Aggregate Loss

Once defined the assets under examination and the types of risks to be measured, the probability and severity distribution should be determined.

Without dedicating too much time to statistical and quantitative aspects, it is worth highlighting that quantitative tools should permit the processing of the following frequency and probability data and information.

The frequency distribution indicates the number of times that the event under examination could occur and the probability of occurrence of each event (Table 6.2).

A severity distribution shows the probability that such an event can cause a certain loss, monetarily measurable, or damage, measurable in different terms (physical damages, reputational damages, business, or supply chain interruptions, etc.).

In the Fig. 6.2, for example, in 90 % of the cases the losses could be between 8,000 and 12,000 Euros.

Two common approaches for risk analysis, which are based on the gravity of a risk, are the estimation of Probable Maximum Loss (PML) and Maximum Foreseeable Loss (MFL).

The PML measures the maximum monetary loss that could probably happen, affecting a business and/or a physical asset. The PML could result from a catastrophe, whether natural or otherwise (the so- called "maximum credible event").

PML is usually expressed as a percentage of the total value, experienced by a structure or collection of structures when subjected to a maximum credible event. This loss estimate is usually smaller than the MFL, which assumes the failure of all active fire and safety protection systems (Table 6.3).

An accurate calculation of PML helps understand risk, analyze the hazards and assess economic losses. It is often used for risks related to natural disasters or risks related to properties, particularly in order to determine the amount of (re)insurance. For example, underwriting decisions could be influenced by PML evaluations, and the amount of (re)insurance provided on a risk could be predicated on the PML evaluation.

In a broader perspective, the probability should also be evaluated, particularly analyzing the probability distribution, as shown in Table 6.4.

The scope is to synthetize both probability and severity data into one value which can represent the entire risk dimension.

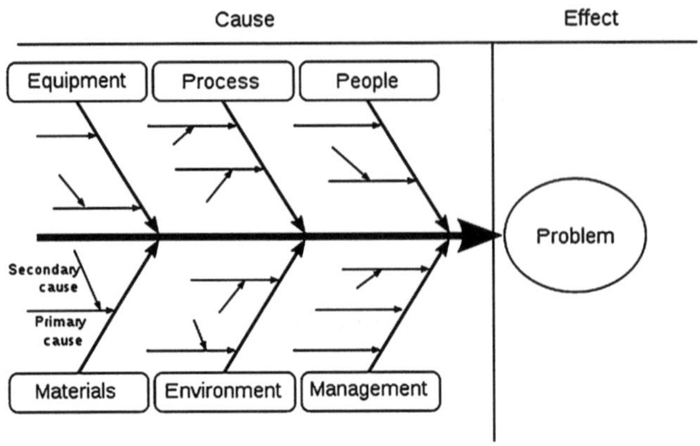


**Fig. 6.2** Case and effect diagram

**Table 6.3** Probability distribution of total losses

| Total losses (in €) | Probability | Cumulative probability |
|---|---|---|
| 0 | 0.10 | 0.10 |
| 1–2,000 | 0.20 | 0.30 |
| 2,001–8,000 | 0.30 | 0.60 |
| 8,001–12,000 | 0.30 | 0.90 |
| 12,001–70,000 | 0.10 | 1.00 |

The MFL is the worst loss that is likely to occur from a single event. A related concept is the Maximum Possible Loss (MPL), typically defined as the worst loss that could possibly occur from of a single event.

An example for considering both the probability and the severity of an event is the calculation of the Annual Probable Maximum Aggregate Loss (APMAL).

Distribution frequency may be described as the value that is equal to or exceeds, within a preset ratio vis-à-vis the total, the yearly total loss resulting from a hazard or a group of hazards.

In other words, APMAL is the largest total loss that a risk unit or a group of risk units is likely to suffer during 1 year. Thus, in the example shown in Table 6.4 we could say that the APMAL at 90 % is 12,000 or 70,000 € thus getting closer to 100 %.

The advantages of APMAL compared to PML may be summarized as follows:

1. Unlike PML, APMAL takes into account not only the severity of the risk, but also its frequency. Therefore, it quantifies a risk in the totality of its dimensional elements.
2. Unlike PML, APMAL also takes into account the fact that the event may not occur and thus allows for a stricter risk assessment.
3. APMAL is a much more flexible concept than PML, because, compared to the latter, it may refer both to a single unit and a group of units exposed to risk.

On the other hand, both APMAL and PML may be calculated in relation to either individual or groups of assets/events.

One of the main problems is the choice of the degree of probability to be allocated to the two measurements. Even though it is impossible to provide an unambiguous answer on this issue, we believe that it should be approximately 90 % or more.

The estimation of APMAL requires the knowledge of the probability distribution of the total yearly losses. This distribution could be empirically developed from the data observed in past experiences. However, the availability of a sufficient number of findings for the distribution to be considered as completely reliable is a rare occurrence. Therefore, in order to solve this problem, some alternative analytical methods were developed and they are grouped in two categories:

2. The first category includes methods that do not require the knowledge of the total yearly loss probability distribution and use statistical measures of data being observed. An example is the "normal approximation technique". This technique assumes that total losses distribution may be approximated by the normal distribution. Therefore, the estimated APMAL would be equal to the expected value of the total loss distribution plus a multiple of its mean square deviation, based on the equation:

$$\text{APMAL} = E(x) + z\sigma(x)$$

where $E(x)$ and $\sigma$ $(x)$ are the average and the mean square deviation, respectively, of the total loss distribution and $z$ is the value of the standardized normal distribution.

The second category includes methods that attempt to estimate this distribution, for example through a computer-based simulation. This technique requires two successive stages and allows the use of both theoretical and empirical distributions of frequency and severity. First, a best estimate is generated and with the frequency distribution you determine how many times the event will occur in the simulation year. Later, additional estimates are generated, one for each time the event will occur. At this stage, with the help of the severity distribution, you can calculate the extent of the loss for each simulated event. Finally, the sum of the losses individually simulated will provide the amount of the total losses for the simulation year.

## 6.4 Qualitative and Semi-Qualitative Methods for Risk Analysis

To put these methods into further context we provide a short description of the best known qualitative and semi-qualitative methods for risk analysis. The objectives are to support the risk analysis, addressing the probability of the event and the severity on the basis of:

- financial losses and cash flow impacts;
- consequences on an organization's competitive edge;
- consequences on customer service;
- consequences on business to business relationships;
- consequences in terms of shareholder and/or customer confidence (and hence the organization's reputation and image);
- consequences affecting employees (lack of engagement and loyalty, de-motivation, etc.);
- consequences on liability to third parties;
- consequences from regulations.

### *6.4.1 Event Tree Analysis and Fault Tree Analysis*

An "event tree" is a graphical representation of the logic model that identifies and quantifies the possible outcomes following an initiating event. Event tree analysis provides an inductive approach to reliability assessment as they are constructed using forward looking logic.

Fault trees use a deductive approach as they are constructed by defining TOP events and then use backward looking logic to define causes. Event tree analysis and fault tree analysis are, however, closely linked. Fault trees are often used to quantify system events that are part of event tree sequences. The logical processes employed to assess event tree sequences and quantify the consequences are same as those used in fault tree analyses (for example see www.eventtreeanalysis.com). Typical TOP events might be, for example, losses of production, safety system unavailability or events such as an explosion. Basic events at the bottom of the fault tree generally represent component and human faults for which statistical failure and repair data is available (components/machinery failures, etc.). The events described in the tree can address both frequency and severity, in order to measure the broader risk dimension.

### *6.4.2 Business Impact Analysis*

Business impact analysis (BIA) typically works through the simulation of a worst-case scenario where business unit and physical structure are destroyed and all assets are not accessible for what would be considered a critical period (e.g., more than 3 weeks).

The business impact analysis is developed in order to estimate the financial and intangible (operational) impacts as a consequence of that worst-case scenario. The scope of this analysis also supports business continuity procedures, in terms of determining the requirements for recovery operations. There are also some applications of BIA as a tool for assessing the upside risk (in terms of assessment of opportunities).

### 6.4.3 Business Continuity Planning (BCP)

Business continuity planning helps organizations prepare and respond to disruptive events—like natural disasters or product delivery interruptions from service providers or suppliers, or simply a significant power outage.

Causes and events related to a disruption should be analyzed and foreseen (where possible), and detailed plans should address those risks in order to ensure appropriate actions during an emergency. BCP is also a risk analysis method as it is utilized to analyze the probability of the disruption and the potential consequences.

### 6.4.4 FMEA

Failure Mode and Effect Analysis (FMEA )is a procedure typically used in operations management to analyze potential failure modes (errors, defects, etc.) in terms of severity and probability of the described failures. It is typically based on the data collected that reflects past experience. The objective is (as is the case with many of the other tools previously mentioned) to balance time and costs dedicated to a potential failure linked to the magnitude of such an event.

### 6.4.5 Dependency Modeling

The objective of dependency modeling is to better address the degree of the risk by simulating the dependence among risks, statistically assessing the potential correlations, creating for this purpose different scenarios related to a dynamically changing environment.

Ishikawa Diagrams (also called fishbone diagrams) are an example of how to represent the correlations of the causes of a certain event (Fig. 6.2). Such analysis supports risk prevention, better assessment of risks, and the analysis of potential factors causing an overall effect.

Each cause of risk may be analyzed as a source of variation. The typical categories of causes include:

- people: anyone involved in the process;
- methods: how the process is performed and the specific requirements for doing it, such as policies, procedures, rules, regulations and laws;
- machines: any equipment, computers, tools, etc. required to carry out the job;
- materials: raw materials, parts, components, molds, dyes, etc. used to produce the final product;
- measurements: data generated from the process that is used to assess its quality;
- environment: the conditions, such as location, time, temperature, and culture in which the process operates.

## 6.5 How Can the Risk Be Assessed when the Historical Data is Insufficient or Lacking?

In the considerations made thus far, we have assumed that the quantity of information drawn from previous corporate experience allows us to determine or at least estimate the frequency distribution, the severity distribution, and the distribution resulting from the total losses.

However, it is a fairly rare occurrence, especially insmall-medium enterprises (SMEs), that sufficient data is available to make these assessments with confidence.

A first method for overcoming the scarcity of sufficient data is to seek out external sources of applicable information. This information, however, has different degrees of accessibility depending on whether it is in the form of published public data (e.g., health-related statistics linked to injuries) or unpublished data (data collected and classified by private entities such as insurers or reinsurers as part of their business).

Finally, other sources of external information may be confidential data available only through independent consultants or insurance brokers and oft times at a cost.

It should be noted that the inference processes based on data drawn from external sources can be even more problematic than those based on insufficient internal data due to the fact that they may not be the best reflection of the organizations specific situation. In any case, prior to their use it is advisable to compare and weigh the internal and external data sets.

We previously discussed how, basically, even when the number of past findings allow us to develop reliable frequency and severity distributions, it is necessary to make a final weighting aimed at reconsidering the elements that affect both the severity and the frequency and that tend to change in a dynamic fashion over the time in which the findings are collected.

This leads us to the understanding, even in very unfavorable situations from a data quantity and quality viewpoint that the final result of the risk measurement may contain significant elements of subjectivity in the allocation of probabilities.

For the person(s) that have to make decisions based on these assessments it is essential to keep in mind that this subjective content naturally increases in inverse proportion to the quantity and quality of the data.

Thus, the weight of the subjective allocations is important when the internal data is scarce and there is a need to rely on external data. In fact, it becomes overwhelming when both the internal and external data is virtually non-existent.

However, making subjective assessments on probability does not mean operating in a merely intuitive fashion. Indeed, there are some techniques that, when used, provide a reasonable hope that allocation errors may be minimized.

**Table 6.4** Risk rating table

| | | | | |
|---|---|---|---|---|
| **Likelihood rating** | | | | |
| 5 | 4 | 3 | 2 | 1 |
| Almost certain | High probability | Possibile | Low probability | Unlikely |
| **Risk Impact rating** | | | | |
| 5 | 4 | 3 | 2 | 1 |
| **Financial - direct loss or opportunity costs of:** | | | | |
| >100m | 50m - 100 m | 25m - 50m | 10m - 25 m | 1 m - 10 m |
| **Operational - missed milestone by:** | | | | |
| > 6 months | 3-6 months | 1-3 months | 1-4 weeks | < 1 week |
| **Regulatory:** | | | | |
| Large scale action, material breach of legislation, with very significant financial or reputational consequences | Regulatory breach with material consequences but which cannot be readly rectified | Regulatory breach with material consequences but which can be readly rectified | Regulatory breach with minimal consequences but which cannot be readly rectified | Regulatory breach with minimal consequences but which can be readly rectified |
| **Strategic / organization - side:** | | | | |
| Failure to meet key strategic objective, organizational variability threatened, major financial overrun | Major impact on strategy, major reputational sensitivity | Moderate impact on strategy, moderate reputational sensitivity | Minor impact on strategy, minor reputational sensitivity | Minimal impact on strategy, minimal reputational sensitivity |
| **Personnel - Loss of managerial staff in 1 year:** | | | | |
| > 30 | >21-30 | > 11-20 | >6-10 | <5 |

## 6.6 Risk Analysis for a Better Performance Improving

The purpose of risk analysis is to determine the extent to which those risks can impair corporate performance. Accordingly, “corporate performance” should be considered both in terms of potential monetary losses and also in terms of underperformance like underperformance in operations, customer service, and other key processes.

### *6.6.1 Risk Analysis for Measuring Monetary Losses*

When the focus is addressing the monetary losses, the scope of the risk analysis is to fill out a risk rating (Table 6.4), where the likelihood of the risk occurring and the potential impact of the risk does occur are assessed.

EVA (Economic Value Added) is a common approach for risk analysis. $\text{EVA} = \text{NOPAT} - \text{Wacc} * \text{CI}$

where

NOPAT = Net Operating Profit After Taxes (more representative in the case of revisional flows)

Wacc = Weighted Average Cost of Capital (this represents the minimum yield demanded by shareholders and creditors);

CI = invested capital

EVA is globally recognized as an insightful way to estimate:

- expected losses which are reasonably estimated (in NOPAT);
- risk exposition and risk appetite (in WACoC).

EVA is otherwise not able to address those risks which are inherent in operations management, in business units and in intangible assets like competitiveness, customer service, or reputation.

These points make EVA an important, but not unique way, to measure risk.

## 6.6.2 Risk Analysis for Measuring Underperformance

An effective Performance Measurement System (PMS) can provide significant support for those organizations that put them in place particularly for risk management and measurement.

PMS supports the organization in monitoring performance against goals, providing boundaries for action, monitoring the efficiency and effectiveness of processes. Hence, an effective PMS can support managers in reducing the unknown risks and properly assessing risk its effects on key processes and value creation.

Risk analysis tools can provide powerful information and guide effective decision making. But a key point is the fact that the selection of the measurement tools can significantly influence the results of the analysis.

In fact, each tool is specifically intended to manage some particular outcomes instead of another: this makes the selection of the tool critical because this can directly influence the power of data analysis.

When analytical tools are introduced as a way to rationally manage complex situations, their selection may influence the priorities in decision-making and the perceptions about the power of business units or functions in the analysis.

Moreover, the information provided is used for reporting and communicating with stakeholders and hence such information may influence external stakeholders.

Therefore it is important for managers to consider, when selecting risk analysis tools, these simple questions:

- what is the objective of risk management and hence of risk analysis?
- what are the priorities in risk management and as a result in risk analysis?
- to whom are you communicating this data and information?
- which role do we want it to play?
- will its characteristics be consistent with its aims?

It is good to keep some of the traditional, well-known *principles for an effective performance management* in mind as a useful guideline in risk management (Franco-Santos et al. 2007; Hall 2008; Neely and Bourne 2000):

- to align measurement perspective with the organization strategic objectives;
- to use a mix of tools, those which can reflect organization priorities and key value drivers;
- to select measures which can be consistent, usable, well understood by managers and stakeholders involved;

- to involve managers and stakeholders who are familiar with the events under analysis;
- to address the cause-and-effect relationships among different measures irrespective of functions and units.

Research published by Dossi and Patelli (2010), based on a study conducted on 144 international organizations, highlighted that in PMS there is a dominance of financial metrics, particularly for the purpose of reporting between headquarters and subsidiaries.

As the authors stated:

> The financial perspective is the most widely adopted measurement perspective in relationships between head- quarters and subsidiaries. The six most frequently reported indicators are related to the financial measurement perspective and capture two critical dimensions of subsidiaries' contributions to global performance, namely financial profitability (the first five indicators in the list: Sales Revenues, Operating Income, Contribution Margin, Gross Margin, Net Income) and capital efficiency (the next two indicators: Cash Flow and Net Working Capital). Consistent with these statistics, the information gathered through interviews rejects the notion of the diminishing importance of financial (typically, accounting) metrics proposed by some early studies on strategic performance measurement (Dossi and Patelli 2010, p. 515).

At the top management level the dominance of financial measurement is commonly related to reporting requirements.

But several other studies and best practices document the emerging role of non-financial indicators in PMS (Neely and Adams 2000). This is consistent with the strategic purpose of PMS, which is also the strategic purpose of risk measurement: supporting strategy implementation, coordinating the different risk taking actions as adopted in separate business units.

Dossi and Patelli's international study noted additional drivers of value creation. These are:

- internal processes;
- human Resources;
- customers.

The study highlighted that these different drivers in the value creation process must be taken into account.

## 6.7 Risk Evaluation

The *risk appetite* and *risk tolerance* of an organization dictate the nature and level of risks that are acceptable to that organization.

Risk appetite could be defined as "the risks that an organization is in business to take, based on its corporate goals and its strategic imperatives." while risk tolerance represents "the threshold of risk that that organization considers acceptable, based on its capabilities to manage the identified risks" (ERM framework 2004).

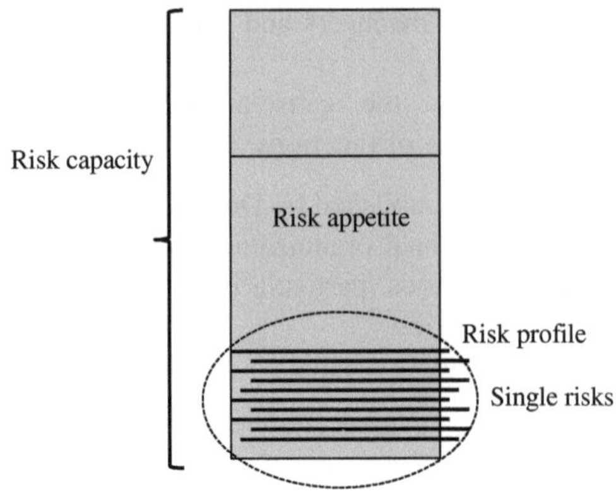


**Fig. 6.3** Risk capacity, risk appetite, risk profile

Risk appetites and tolerances can vary according to the balance of opportunity, uncertainty or hazard which different risks represent.

Some organizations produce a "risk appetite statement" which represents a sort of "vision" about their risk management approach that is applicable to all classes of risk.

As AIRMIC-SARM-IRM stated: "It is fairly easy for an organization to confirm that it has no appetite for causing injury and ill health. In practice, however, this may need to be developed into a set of targets for health and safety performance. There is a danger that risk appetite statements fail to be dynamic, and they can constrain behavior and rapid response".

The concept of risk appetite could be analyzed differently depending on the perspective of the evaluator:

- at Board level, risk appetite is a driver of strategic risk decisions.
- at executive level, risk appetite translates into a set of procedures to ensure that risk receives adequate attention when making tactical decisions.
- at operational level, risk appetite dictates operational constraints for routine activities.

In other words, the company should define a *risk capacity*, as the maximum risk that the company could accept, defining (within the risk capacity) the *risk appetite*, as the amount of risk the Group is willing to accept in pursuing value creation.

The risk appetite should be defined on the basis of the *risk profile*, which is the aggregation of single risks (Fig. 6.3).

Moreover, it should be highlighted that the personnel risk aversion or risk attitude depends on the activities and responsibilities of the employees. While the board may have typically a "risk taker" profile, the middle management is more risk-adverse. This is due to the fact that the strategic area is focused on the capability to seize opportunities lying in risks (upside risks), while the organizational area is focused on the prevention and protection from negative events (downside risks) (Fig. 6.4).

Once risks are analyzed, there is the need to compare the measured risk with the risk criteria, established by the organization: this is the risk evaluation.

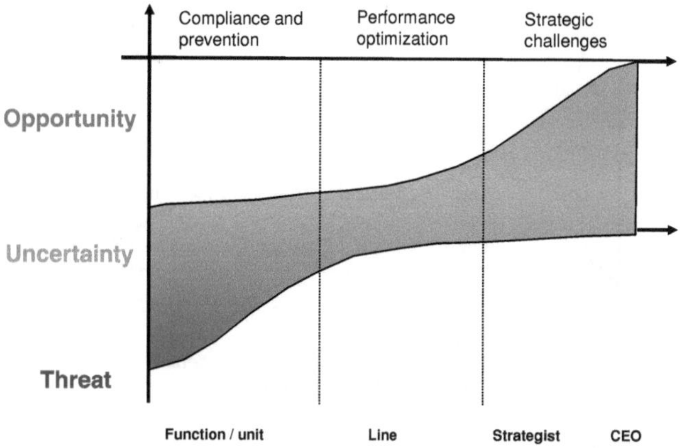


**Fig. 6.4** Risk perception in the organization. *Source* Price water house coopers

ISO 31000 (2009). 2.24 Risk Evaluation
Risk evaluation is a process that is used to compare risk analysis results with risk criteria in order to determine whether or not a specified level of risk is acceptable or tolerable.

Risk criteria represent the level of risk that the organization sets out as "acceptable" or "non-acceptable" (hence treatable) and are, as stated by ISO 31.000, point 2.22: "terms of reference used to evaluate the significance or importance of your organization's risks. They are used to determine whether a specified level of risk is acceptable or tolerable.

Risk criteria should reflect your organization's values, policies, and objectives, should be based on its external and internal context, should consider the views of stakeholders, and should be derived from standards, laws, policies, and other requirements."

The process of risk evaluation allows the managers to represent risks within a matrix as shown in Fig. 6.5. In that representation, risks can be classified on the basis of their priority and nature of actions required.

This classification can be made with major details by adding a set of qualitative and quantitative data to be collected and compared.

Information like probability and severity could be integrated with useful information from other.

"measures" such as:

- predictability;
- potential effect on the organization key performance indicators;
- the quality of processes, systems and cultural controls put in place to mitigate these risks.

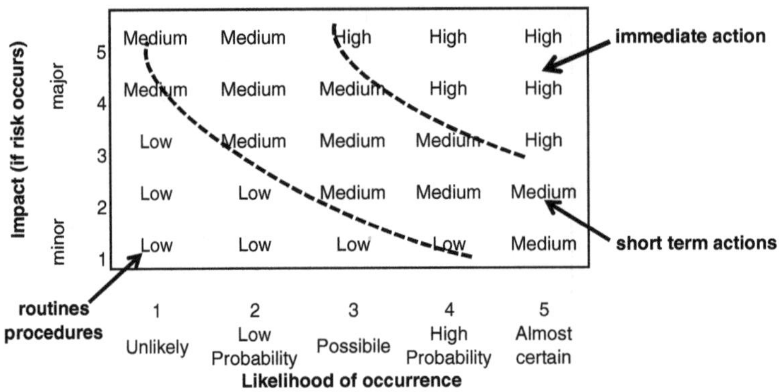


**Fig. 6.5** Risks classified by priorities

**Table 6.5** Risk evaluation by priority

| Risk | Probability | Severity | Quality of controls | Key objectives involved | Score (1–5) |
|---|---|---|---|---|---|
| Judgment | (high, mean, low) | (high, mean, low) | (high, mean, low) | (high, mean, low) | (1–5) |
| *Risk a* | H | L | M | M | 2.5 |
| *Risk b* | M | M | L | H | 4.8 |
| *Risk c* | M | L | H | M | 1.5 |
| ... | | | | | |

These measures provide qualitative and subjective information, but could be combined and processed into a number, like a score on a scale of 1 (low) to 5 (high). This score is a sort of weight of the risk, and allows the senior management to manage those risks more effectively (see Table 6.5).

The results from risk analysis and risk evaluation support the organization in building risk profiles, prioritizing risk treatment efforts, allocating the necessary budget in order to invest in control in an effective and efficient way. This topic is described when addressing the concepts of Cost of Risk.

## 6.8 External contribution 6.1: Analysis of Economic, Financial and Equity Indicators for the Assessment of Business Risk and Client Risk in an Industrial Group

The O.R.I. Martin Group is specialized in high quality long products steel production and is divided in different product units depending on the type of products, like special steels for mechanical applications and construction steels, and markets.

**Risk Assessment**

The key business risk drivers are fundamentally identifiable under four macro areas:

1. *Sales Area*
   - Clients risk;
   - Responsibility for products sold;
   - Risk from competition and export markets.
2. *Supply Area*
   - Suppliers risk;
   - Commodity volatility;
   - Capacity of supplying with the factors of production used.
3. *Financial area*
   - Financing source balance;
   - Interest rate trends;
   - Exchange rate trends.
4. *Safety area*
   - Safety at work;
   - Fire and catastrophic events;
   - Environmental disasters.

In order to analyse the clients risk, reference is made to the analysis of the financial statements of the last five financial years.

The analysis is carried out according to the following phases:

- analysis of financial statements (income statement and statement of assets and liabilities);
- financial flow analysis (statement of account);
- analysis of the composition of capital invested and of financial sources;
- analysis of economic and financial ratios.

The analytical approach described above is based on the data that is official but is not immediately available since the time for financial statements to be approved and filed involve a data delay of about 6–9 months; for this reason the Group, in order to be quickly updated on the situation of its clients and monitor the development of clients risk in the short-term, uses the following means:

- regular meetings with clients for situation updates (regarding orders, business profitability, …);
- information collected via sales staff (and possibly agents) on the market;
- use of business information and credit insurance;
- in areas deemed to be high risk, the Group only works with letter of credits that have been counter-guaranteed by an Italian bank.

Another risk factor perceived by the Group and which has become even more significant in recent months is the so-called "Country" risk, i.e., the risk of a State finding itself in a condition where it cannot meet the financial commitments made by its residents toward non-resident entities due to a lack of resources or for whatever other reason (political unrest, natural disasters, etc.).

The objective is to limit the "Country" risk of the business counterpart as far as possible. To manage this aspect, specialized analysis agency reports and payment instruments counter-guaranteed by Italian banks are used, or by supplies are carried out only against advances made by the client.

The Group, in analysing its clients risk, uses an analysis of economic, financial, and equity indicators.

Starting from the reclassification of the income statement and statement of assets and liabilities, the Group calculates a series of indicators (economic, financial, and equity indicators) to have the possibility of creating a company overview in order to derive useful information for the relations that the company maintains.

It is essential in any case to take a holistic approach to business analysis, since only a broad analysis that is developed, where possible, by reading the documents accompanying the financial statements, such as the Management Report and Explanatory Notes, allows useful indications for the management to be obtained.

In the case of the O.R.I. Martin Group's analytical approach, the following aspects are analyzed using the indicators mentioned above.

*Assets strength*

- *Fixed assets coverage index of Net Equity*, indicating the extent to which the fixed assets are financed using shareholder's equity, where for ratios greater than or equal to 1, the fixed assets are covered by the business's permanent resources.
- *Financial Independence Index*, which highlights the degree of business self financing relating the shareholder's financial resources with the total of both fixed and current investments. The threshold value is 30; below 30 % the company may be undercapitalised.

*Analysis of financial management*

- *Liquidity index*, which measures the company's capacity to pay the debts which are due in the short-term, not taking into account the resources generated from warehouse stocks. The company demonstrates a satisfactory level of liquidity where the index has a value greater than or equal to 1. For values less than 1, to address the current liabilities it may be necessary to sell off the warehouse stocks or fixed assets.
- *Availability index*, which measures the company's capacity to pay the short-term debts using cash or quickly available liquidity, also taking the resource generating from warehouse stocks into account. A value between 1 and 2 can be considered satisfactory depending on warehouse stocks incidence and the time needed to convert it into cash.

- *Financial Charges Coverage index* indicates how many times the operating result (EBIT) can be reduced before the company is no longer able to pay its financial debts. Values exceeding 1.5 are considered satisfactory.

*Monetary cycle*:

- The *duration of the monetary cycle* depends on a series of factors: the average time in stock of the materials, average delay obtained from suppliers, duration of the production technical cycle, average time in stock of finished products, and average delay conceded to clients. In the analysis of the rotation indices, the dynamics of turnover growth, the incidence of taxation policy (VAT) and that of situations generated by overdue takings remain uncollected. The warehouse rotation rate is calculated with reference to the purchases of the period.

*Analysis of the profitability of the net equity*

- The *ROE* measures the return on the shareholder's equity, i.e., the level of remuneration of the capital purchased with the bond of full risk. The ROE is an indicator of profitability and as such can be compared with the return on alternative investments. We should remember that the ROE can be broken down as follows: "ROE = (ROI—Financial charges/borrowed capital) * Risk rate + ROI + incidence of Extraordinary Management and Tax Management".
- The *ROI* expresses the return of the capital invested into the company net of the investments outside normal operations.
- *The Financial Charges Index/Borrowed Capital* measures the average cost of financing sources made available by third parties to the company.
- The *Risk Rate* expresses the amount of debt compared to that of net equity against the total of sources which the company has used. It provides an expected estimate of the risk which characterizes the position of the creditors.
- The *Financial Leverage* can be defined as the action exerted by financial policy on business profitability: Financial Leverage = (ROI—Financial debts/Borrowed Capital) * Risk Rate. As long as the ROI exceeds the cost of the debts, the financial structure has a positive effect and is advantageous.
- The *Incidence of extraordinary items + taxes* measures the impact of extraordinary management and tax management with regard to the net equity invested in the company.

*Analysis of the Financial Report*

- The aim of the *Financial Report* is to analyze all the financial flows that have taken place during all of the business activities (operational, investment, financial, tax, extraordinary) during the course of the financial year. The financial statement shows all of the variations in the invested capital and the financing sources. Analysing the financial report allows understanding the ways in which financial resources are obtained and how these resources have been used.

*Debt analysis*

- *Debt/Net Income* is one of the main indices monitored by credit institutions in business analyzes and measures the ratio between the company's debt and turnover.
- The *Risk Rate* expresses the amount of debt with regard to that of the net equity against the total of the financing sources that the business has used. It provides an expected estimate of the risk which characterizes the position of creditors.

*Z-Score analysis*

- The analysis developed by *Prof. Edward I. Altman* during the 1960s still plays an important role today in the assessment of businesses. The reason for its success lies in the ease of understanding and use of the model; the analysis is carried out on the balance sheet and requires a simple mathematical calculation.

*Economic Value Added Analysis*

- The Economic Value Added measures a company's capacity to create or destroy value. It measures the management's ability to make the capital invested exceed the sources that finance it.

The concept of Weighted Average Cost of Capital (WACC) is fundamental in the analysis of this methodological approach; it is a term which identifies the average cost of resources used in the company and must be compared with the income generated by the invested capital.

*Corporate Profile*

The O.R.I. Martin Group, over the course of recent years and even following the serious global crisis of world economy of 2008, has been characterized by a satisfying earnings capacity and an optimum capitalisation, and therefore in 2011 arrived at a turnover of EUR 462,228 and a net equity of EUR 164,720.

The Group has production facilities in Italy and the United States as well as Sales Offices in major European counties. As regards export markets, 63 % of the revenue comes from the domestic market while the Group's business partner is Germany.

## 6.9 External contribution 6.2: Risk Management and Valuation: A Board Issue

As said in the Introduction to the International Rule ISO 31000 *Risk Management—Principles and guidelines, "All activities of an organization involve risk"*. In a scenery of political and economic uncertainty, or in contexts with a globalized *supply chain*, risks multiply and time to decide shortens dramatically.

*A critical situation*

More than in other European countries, the use of the appraisal as a decisional tool is often underrated. The insurance valuation of the fixed assets—when considered—is perceived as a commodity, while the valuation—and the insurance—of the losses deriving from business interruption is a privilege of no more than 5 % of the companies, although the business interruption is the first cause of bankruptcy.

In transactions or in financial operations, as well, little attention is paid to the value of the fixed assets and to their capacity of granting a prosecution of the usual production, while the interest is focused on the financial perspective of the companies involved: but how to minimize the effects of an uncertain situation, where the market is instable or, sometimes, non-existent? How banks can avoid the risk of a non-performing loan? Could a private equity eliminate the risk of growing post-acquisition maintenance expenditures?

The lack of a common terminology among the different stakeholders, the unplugged gaps in the local and the international regulations involving the asset management (IAS/IFRS, US GAAP, SOX, etc.) do not facilitate the birth of a real "culture" of the value and of the risk.

*To know the impact makes the business less vulnerable*

A professional appraisal can represent an essential tool, when:

- insuring the fixed assets against the material damages;
- assuring the business continuity;
- choosing a supplier or a partner;
- selling shares, assets and businesses;
- asking for a loan;
- contributing in a joint venture.

In fact, the choice of using this instrument not only shows a will of transparency and a long-sightedness, but also provides a basis for a fair discussion, and—by means of specific policies—implies a real transfer of responsibility to a third, professional and independent party.

*The insurance appraisal*

The twin perils of over and under insurance are avoided by an accurate valuation assessment of the sums insured. Over insurance results in excessive premiums. Under insurance, while delivering cheaper premiums, can be disastrous, with the failure of insurers to pay out sums sufficient to reinstate the assets of a business, or to compensate for business interruption, frequently resulting in wider business failures. An independent appraisal eliminates the most part of the discussions connected to a loss settlement.

*The market valuation*

Appraisers are called to carry out a valuation of the assets with a view of determining their fair market value, taking into consideration the following factors:

- Date of purchase;
- Type of asset and extent of use (general purpose or specific);
- Repairs and maintenance policy of the enterprise;
- Availability of spare parts in the future;
- Future demand for the product manufactured by an asset.

The IAS "fair value"—a theoretic value, for financial use only—has represented a real question mark for the appraisers: the elusive definition and methodology permitted a wide range of interpretations. On January 1st, 2013, the newly adopted IFRS 13 will—finally—provide clear and consistent guidance for measuring it, addressing valuation uncertainty in markets that are no longer active and defining an identical wording for IFRSs and US GAAP to increase transparency in cross-border transactions. For the first time, classes of assets and liabilities will be determined on the basis of their nature, characteristics, and *risks.*

*A tool for corporate decision makers*

Born "to serve and serve you well whenever you feel the need of such service" (*Company mission statement,* February 1, 1896). We are focused on appraisal and value since over a century. Our main goal is to create a "culture of value", allowing us to share our experience and methodologies with a competent, well-informed customer.

But it's not only of matter of value: more and more often we are called to detect functional and economic obsolescence of the assets, within M&A operations. In fact, the risks in purchasing a business are often hidden in the maintenance and running costs, not correctly forecasted/measured at the moment of the purchase.

A recent assignment concerning an oil refinery resulted in the decision of not closing the deal when our study—after having considered the size, the complexity, the product range, the age of the assets, the technology and the market—highlighted a reduced productive capacity in comparison with a new plant, an increase of the energetic costs and a huge demand of investment deriving from a previous lack of extraordinary maintenance. In fact, significant technological advances have been made in technology, energy conservation, and process configuration over the years which a prudent investor must consider if constructing a refinery today, the use of new technology resulting in higher production yields, increased control, reduced labor requirements and utility costs, reduced chemical and catalyst expense, and greater operating flexibility.

*Corporate Profile*

American Appraisal is the largest full-service independent valuation consulting firm in the world with a global network of offices and staff positioned to serve our clients, both large and small.

Founded in 1896, American Appraisal was established with the aim of setting up supportable insurance values across the United States. In this period since we have continued to focus our efforts on the insurance market, while spreading the reach of our services.

We can assist our clients by providing:

- detailed insurance valuation studies;
- market valuations;
- IAS/IASB valuation ("Fair value");
- M&A financial valuation and consultancy;
- technical Advisory/Due Diligence;
- property record services;
- export certification.

## References

Dossi A, Patelli L (2010) You learn from what you measure: financial and non-financial performance measures in multinational companies. Long Range Plan 43(2010):498–526

Hassett MJ (1999) Probability for risk management. Actex Publications, Winsted

Jorion P (2001) Value at risk: the new benchmark for managing financial risk. McGraw-Hill, New York

Neely A, Adams CA (2000) Perspective on performance: the performance prism, Centre for Business Performance-Cranfield University, Cranfield-Bedford

Neely A, Bourne M (2000) Why measurement initiatives fail. Meas Bus Excell 4(4):3–7

Pawitan Y (2001) In all likelihood: statistical modeling and inference using likelihood. Oxford University Press, Oxford

Wilson R (2001) Risk-benefit analysis. Harvard Centre for Risk Analysis, Cambridge

# Appendix to Part II

| Checklist for risk management | |
|---|---|
| Category: Customer risk | |
| **Source of risk** | **Ideas for risk reduction** |
| Meeting customer expectations (no matter how precise the terms of reference, there are typically countless questions of interpretation) | Use customer mapping technique to organize what you know about the customer organization and its key players |
| | Obtain samples of previous work that was considered satisfactory or similar systems and use these as a benchmark to gauge expectations |
| | Prepare and present expanded tables of contents and page counts as early as possible |
| | Present samples of similar deliverables produced in accordance with the same standards |
| | Meet regularly with the Acceptor |
| | Use decision request and change request procedures to maintain a record of all related discussions and control all changes relative to the schedule and cost |
| | Maintain a record of all time spent resolving these factors |
| | Hold regular Steering Committee meetings |
| Managing senior management perceptions | Ensure active involvement of a steering committee, so that:<br>• Customer management rather than the project team sets the direction for the project;<br>• The continuous, regular involvement of customer management generates commitment;<br>• All issues discussed and resolved increase the user comfort factor |
| Political risk | Assess organizational readiness:<br>• Is senior management committed to the project to ensure that it gets appropriate priority and support?<br>• Do the management and staff perceive that this project will improve the organization and/or the environment in which people work?<br>• Is there a champion with adequate influence who strongly supports the project, to the extent that he/she is willing to fight to have the project succeed?<br>• Are people, computer capacity, money and other resources available to implement the project effectively or are there other competing demands for resources that will receive higher priority? |
| | Do the staff members involved in the project have the necessary skills to implement the project? |
| | Set up a network to gather intelligence on what the key people are talking about—who speaks to whom, when and why, any issues that may be developing, etc. |
| | Use change influences analysis and resistance management techniques to analyze and address driving and opposing forces |
| | Prepare specific commitment strategies and plans to obtain political support |

(continued)

A. Borghesi and B. Gaudenzi, *Risk Management*, Perspectives in Business Culture,
DOI: 10.1007/978-88-470-2531-8, © Springer-Verlag Italia 2013

| Checklist for risk management | |
|---|---|
| Category: Customer risk | |
| **Source of risk** | **Ideas for risk reduction** |
| | Establish overwhelming commitment to success at the executive level so that thoughts of failure are not permitted |
| | Ensure key opinion leaders are directly involved in the project team |
| | Lobby for votes ahead of time to ensure that you know the outcome of key meetings before you go in |
| Changing requirements | Define scope up front in measurable terms:<br>• Horizontal scope;<br>• Vertical scope (which defines the amount of functionality to be automated versus the functionality to be addressed manually);<br>• The limits to be applied to unbounded tasks;<br>• Other estimating assumptions;<br>• The acceptance criteria. |
| | Design for information "hiding" to confine impact of likely changes and minimize their impact on the rest of the system |
| | Plan incremental development, deferring changes to later increments |
| Inaccurate or insufficient detail in requirements statement | Build in realistic time for confirmation of requirements |
| | Include limiting assumptions in contract |
| Inability of user to define requirements or ever-expanding scope | Build prototype |
| | Limit number of reviews of deliverables |
| | Include provision in contract for replacement of Acceptor if scope undefined by specified milestone |
| | Include provision for termination of contract if scope undefined by specified milestone |
| Goldplating (desire to over automate) | Establish a budget constraint to focus the effort on where there will be most payback and to force decisions that otherwise would be avoided, including early clarification of major scope issues. With reasonable constraints, a system design is apt to be spare and clean whereas without these, functionality that could be handled on an exception basis is likely to be added into the system design causing the cost and implementation effort to increase dramatically. Typically, even if the system lives through to implementation, only a fraction of such functionality is regularly used |
| | Conduct scope review at start of project |
| | Conduct a cost/benefit analysis |
| | Assign each function a value in an appropriate currency (time, $, m bytes of memory, n microseconds per invocation, etc.) |
| | Scrub requirements and remove unessential |
| | Design and develop to cost |
| Cost is too high | Use Steering Committee to negotiate scope reduction |
| | Design/develop to cost |
| | Incremental development (versions) |
| | Scrub requirements and remove unessential |

(continued)

(continued)

| Checklist for risk management | |
|---|---|
| Category: Customer risk | |
| Source of risk | Ideas for risk reduction |
| | Consider software reuse<br>Consider productivity tools<br>Minimize formal deliverables and substitute with working papers |
| Pressure for an early completion date | More rigorous up-front planning. Use the WBS for time-reduction analysis. Look for "work-ahead" items that can be started early<br>Design/develop to schedule<br>Develop incrementally (versions)<br>Scrub requirements and remove unessential<br>Consider software reuse<br>Consider productivity tools<br>Minimize formal deliverables and substitute with working papers<br>Use a more experienced team<br>Build an excellent infrastructure and SDE well in advance<br>Add schedule management to the formal risk management plan to ensure visibility, and pro-actively address schedule variances<br>Minimize any changes during the project time frame which may impact the project (e.g., changes to project staff, customer policies and procedures)<br>Collocate team for maximum productivity |
| Lack of user commitment | Obtain executive commitment to provide adequate end-user participation<br>Clearly define specific areas of user responsibility<br>Raise the visibility of customer dependencies at the Steering Committee<br>Appoint a user co-ordinator<br>Set up an Implementation Advisory Group to get a broad range of users involved in acceptance testing, training, user documentation, implementation roll-out, etc.<br>Develop a plan for ensuring user understanding (e.g., user surveys)<br>Ensure user awareness of all issues through regular status reports and sign-offs<br>Arrange for user involvement in analysis workshops and prototyping<br>Highlight user responsibility for an Acceptance Test, involving the thorough retesting of all system functions<br>Highlight user sign-offs which put emphasis on the user confirming that they understand or complaining when they don't |
| Lack of continuity of key players | Implement key personnel agreements and contractual provisions |
| Specifying requirements that are difficult or impossible to meet | Staff analysts who are experts in the business area and skilled at negotiating better ways of solving the business problem |

(continued)

(continued)

| Checklist for risk management | |
|---|---|
| Category: Customer risk | |
| Source of risk | Ideas for risk reduction |
| | Use "flying squads" of credible business, application and technology specialists to resolve areas of conflict |
| User training and acceptance | Set up an Implementation Advisory Group to get a broad range of users involved in acceptance testing, training, user documentation, implementation roll-out, etc. |
| | Develop a training program and accompanying training plan |
| | Install a training infrastructure (e.g., help desk, toll-free telephone support) |
| Achievement of customer's projected return on investment | Reduce exposure by breaking large projects into several smaller ones |
| | Sequence projects so that those with tangible benefits are completed first |

| Checklist for risk management | |
|---|---|
| Category: Technical (product) risk | |
| Source of risk | Ideas for risk reduction |
| Developing the wrong system (i.e., shortfalls in functionality) | Mission analysis: study how the organization performs its mission to enable informed judgement on information requirements |
| | User surveys |
| | High level of end-user participation |
| | Benchmark the "best practices" in equivalent systems elsewhere |
| | Build prototype |
| | Write user aids early |
| | Ensure that a contract is in place which clearly defines scope and deliverables |
| Shortfalls in the user interface | User engineering: study how the user works to gain better understanding of the requirements for the user interface |
| | Build prototype |
| | Write scenarios |
| Unknown future changes | Design for information "hiding" to confine impact of likely changes and minimize their impact on the rest of the system |
| Compatibility of technical components | Build technical prototype |
| Version changes in third-party software over the life of the project | Implement formal risk management techniques and risk tracking/reporting procedures |
| Shortfalls in externally supplied components (performance, stability, reliability, robustness, etc.) | Benchmarking |
| | Inspections |

(continued)

(continued)

| Checklist for risk management | |
|---|---|
| Category: Technical (product) risk | |
| Source of risk | Ideas for risk reduction |
| | Reference checking |
| Lack of availability of components | Contingency planning |
| Overall system performance (end to end) | Implement formal risk management techniques and risk tracking/reporting procedures |
| | "Buy information"—i.e., invest in additional data gathering |
| | Apply capacity planning/analysis techniques (e.g., CRYSTAL, TPNS) |
| | Build in contractual protection |
| Unknown sizing data or gaps in understanding of volumetric data | Implement formal risk management techniques and risk tracking/reporting procedures |
| Uncertainty in projections or calculations | Implement formal risk management techniques and risk tracking/reporting procedures |
| Quality of the delivered product | Involve the team in defining standards in advance |
| | Ensure that standards are formally documented, easily accessible, and easily understandable |
| | Provide early feedback on adherence to standards |
| | Include adherence to standards as an item in walk-throughs |

| Checklist for risk management | |
|---|---|
| Category: Delivery risk | |
| Source of risk | Ideas for risk reduction |
| Personnel shortfalls (people and qualifications) | Staff with top talent |
| | Use overqualified staff in critical situations |
| | Replace junior team members with more expensive but more productive staff |
| | Consider external sources (e.g., subcontract) |
| | Implement key personnel agreements for critical resources |
| | Share resources or provide shadow/assistants to minimize the time demand on key resources that are also in demand for other work |
| | Provide comprehensive orientation (account, proposal, internal and customer objectives, application, technology, customer, etc.) |
| | Provide additional technical training under the direction of the technical architect |

(continued)

(continued)

| Checklist for risk management | |
|---|---|
| Category: Delivery risk | |
| Source of risk | Ideas for risk reduction |
| | Bring in special project "start-up" teams to get the team up and running |
| Unrealistic project plan (schedules and budget) | Have independent estimators prepare detailed task-based estimates and apply sanity checks |
| | Use experience with sample programs (e.g., program models) to validate proposed productivity rates |
| | Ensure that the estimates are "owned" by the people who will be responsible to deliver to them |
| | Design/develop to cost |
| | Price by phase, not whole project |
| | Incremental development |
| | Software reuse |
| | Requirements scrubbing |
| | Assume risk in starting early |
| Project management | Consider nature of customer in estimating amount of project management time required |
| | Implement the project management techniques in the knowledge base |
| | Use overqualified project manager in critical situations |
| | Ensure that resolution of all issues and problems are assigned to individuals and documented in decision requests, information requests, etc. |
| Customer management | Implement basic techniques such as steering committee, status reporting, CR, DR and IR procedures, as defined in the knowledge base |
| | Implement activity assignment and progress tracking for customer responsibilities |
| | Raise the visibility of customer dependencies at the steering committee (have these routinely reviewed) |
| | Implement formal risk management techniques and risk tracking/reporting procedures |
| | Implement formal problem resolution procedures |
| Problems with the acceptor role (no acceptor identified, inappropriate acceptor, or multiple acceptors) | Work with the customer executive to identify an appropriate acceptor |
| | Increase the visibility of the project organization chart (the "H" format) with the project manager and acceptor and make sure the communication channels are clearly identified |

(continued)

(continued)

| Checklist for risk management | |
|---|---|
| Category: Delivery risk | |
| Source of risk | Ideas for risk reduction |
| Committed team | Ensure personal and project objectives have been reconciled |
| | Ensure that project management fundamentals have been applied (project model, visibility, accountability and confidence) |
| | Ensure that the cycle of delegate, witness commitment, and monitor commitment is adhered to |
| | Individual weekly review of days ahead/behind schedule with each team member |
| | Weekly team meetings, as appropriate, to facilitate team communication, develop team spirit, and allow issues to be discussed at the team level on a scheduled basis rather than in interrupt mode |
| | Provide productivity tools |
| | Focus on team member chemistry |
| | Motivate for performance |
| | Rotate through project roles, where appropriate, to increase team member responsibilities and provide career development opportunities |
| | Coach poor performers |
| | Replace poor performers if necessary |
| New/unknown technology | Consider external sources (e.g., sub-contract) |
| | Provide for training |
| Subcontractor capability | Pre-qualify sub-contractors using interviews and formal assessment methodology (e.g., SEI assessment methodology from Carnegie Mellon University) |
| | Conduct reference checks |
| | Require competitive construction of prototype |
| | Conduct pre-award audit |
| | Check references (and personal commitment level) |
| | Substitution clause in contract with repayment for time lost |
| | Specify conditions and remedy in event of poor performance |
| | Plan for early delivery and include contingency plans for if delivery is missed |
| Subcontractor ability to deliver as planned | Ensure delivery schedule is included in sub-contract |
| | Ensure that sub-contractor's and prime contractor's delivery schedules coincide |

(continued)

(continued)

| Checklist for risk management | |
|---|---|
| Category: Delivery risk | |
| Source of risk | Ideas for risk reduction |
| | Base payment on appropriate milestones |
| | Use holdbacks |
| | Obtain authority to be responsible for the formal performance reviews of the individuals concerned for their work on the project |
| Customer ability to meet its delivery commitments | Specify conditions and remedy in event of poor performance |
| | Plan for early delivery and include contingency plans for if delivery is missed |
| | Obtain authority to be responsible for the formal performance reviews of the individuals concerned for their work on the project |
| | Routinely raise the visibility of customer performance to plan at the steering committee meeting |
| Phase gaps | Include in contract negotiations |
| Acceptance delays | Use basic techniques such as steering committee, status reporting, CR, DR and IR procedures, to ensure visibility |
| Decision delays | Implement basic techniques such as steering committee, status reporting, CR, DR and IR procedures, to ensure visibility |
| Uncontrolled meeting time | Establish a meeting protocol ahead of time, for example:<br>• Effort will be made to limit the number of meetings and minimize the number of attendees at all meetings;<br>• All scheduled meetings will require a specific agenda of matters for discussion to be prepared and distributed in advance;<br>• Meeting duration will be stated in advance and respected;<br>• All scheduled meetings will result in a brief summary of matters resolved and decisions and action plans resulting. |
| External factors (e.g., strike at customer facilities) | Contingency planning |
| | Contractual protection |

*Source* C. Borysowich, Risk Management Checklist, Jan 26, 2008, it.toolbox.com/blogs/enterprise-solutions/risk-management-checklist-22039

## Risk assessment in your pocket: tips and tricks

This is a short list of actions that summarizes the contents of Part II; more details are available in the chapters.

**Table A.1** Planning and designing the risk context

| Identify | Concepts, tools and techniques | Questions |
|---|---|---|
| Key objectives | Shareholder value<br>Customer service<br>Efficiency<br>... | How can risks impact these objectives? |
| Key processes | Production<br>Service provision<br>Procurement<br>... | Which are the key risks affecting these processes? |
| Key stakeholders | Customers<br>Decision-makers<br>Employees<br>Financial institutions<br>... | Who are the key stakeholders? How can risks impact on their expectations? |
| Risk management: Scope | Business risk management and/or Enterprise risk management | What is the objective of risk management? |
| Risk management: architecture | Business risk management and/or enterprise risk management | What are the principles, framework and techniques? Who is the risk owner? How are roles and responsibilities allocated? |

**Table A.2** Risk description

| | |
|---|---|
| Risk name | Unique identifier or risk index |
| Risk scope | Define the scope of risk and details of possible events, including description of the events, their size, type and number |
| Risk nature | Classify risk, timescale of potential impact and describe as hazard, opportunity or uncertainty.<br>Is the impact strategic, operational, and financial? |
| Stakeholders | Identify stakeholders, both internal and external, and their expectations |
| Risk analysis | Assess probability and magnitude: Which method of analysis is involved (qualitative–quantitative)? |
| Loss experience | Are there previous incidents and prior loss experience of events related to the risk? |
| Risk tolerance, appetite or attitude | Loss potential and anticipated financial impact of the risk;<br>Target for risk control and desired level of performance;<br>Define risk attitude, appetite, tolerance or limits for the risk. |
| Risk response, treatment and controls | Evaluate existing control mechanisms and activities, and the level of confidence in existing controls.<br>Define procedures for monitoring and review risk performance. |

(continued)

**Table A.2** (continued)

| | |
|---|---|
| Potential for risk improvement | Define potential for cost-effective risk improvement or modification;<br>Define recommendations, milestones and deadlines for implementation;<br>Define responsibility for implementing any improvements. |
| Strategy and policy developments | Define responsibility for developing strategy related to the risk.<br>Define responsibility for auditing compliance with controls. |

**Table A.3** Likelihood and consequences

| When a risk is… | …its likelihood is… |
|---|---|
| Is expected to occur in most circumstances | Almost certain |
| Will probably occur in most circumstances | Likely |
| Might occur at some time and may be difficult to control due to some external influences | Possible |
| Could occur some time | Unlikely |
| may occur only in exceptional circumstances | rare |
| *When a risk generates these financial and/or operational consequences…* | *…its severity is…* |
| −15 % of monthly budget &/or $1,000,000 limit.<br>Total systems dysfunction. Critical shutdown of operations. | Critical |
| −10 % of monthly budget &/or $500,000 limit.<br>All operational areas of a location or region jeopardized. Other locations/regions may be affected. | Extreme |
| −5 % of monthly budget &/or $ 100,000 limit.<br>Disruption to a number of operational areas within a location or region & possible flow onto other locations/regions. | Major |
| −2 % of monthly budget &/or $40,000 limit<br>Some disruption manageable by altered operational routine. | Minor |

*Source* Adapted from Knight 2010

**Table A.4** Priorities in management

| | | Severity | | |
|---|---|---|---|---|
| | | Very high | Medium | Very low |
| Likelihood | Highly likely | Priority 1 | Priority 1 | *Priority 2* |
| | Possible | Priority 1 | *Priority 2* | Priority 3 |
| | Unlikely/rare | *Priority 2* | Priority 3 | Priority 3 |

# Part III
# Risk Treatment: Approaches, Techniques and Good Practices

# Chapter 7
# Risk Treatment

We can describe risk treatment as a complex activity aimed at modifying and/or mitigating risks and the potential economic and financial impact of such risks through risk control and risk financing actions.

As we drill down further we can define risk control as acting on the two main factors or risk, i.e., frequency and severity. In parallel we add the definition of risk financing: mitigating the economic and/or financial effects of risks so that, if an event has indeed occurred, the economic and/or financial consequences of the loss are reduced (Dionne 2000, Haefeli and Liedtke 2012).

Hence, risk treatment (control and financing) encompasses all the options available for treating those risks which are considered as intolerable during the phase of risk assessment. A further definition of risk treatment is provided by ISO 31000 and is described here below.

> ISO 31000 (2009). 5.5.1. Risk treatment
> Risk treatment involves selecting one or more options for modifying risks and implementing those options. Once implemented, treatments provide or modify the controls.

The treatment options are identified in Fig. 7.1.

## 7.1 Risk Control

Risk Control aims at reducing the frequency and severity of losses and making losses more predictable. Risk control is particularly suitable for treating unforeseen and fortuitous losses. It is therefore the main objective of the previously mentioned risk control actions to protect human and organizational resources, subject to these losses.

We can look at these options in more detail below:

A. Borghesi and B. Gaudenzi, *Risk Management*, Perspectives in Business Culture,
DOI: 10.1007/978-88-470-2531-8_7, © Springer-Verlag Italia 2013 

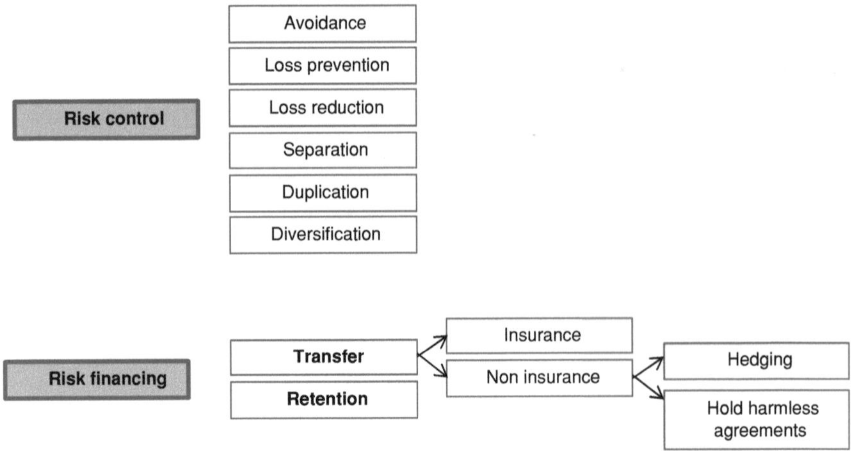


**Fig. 7.1** Risk treatment options

### *7.1.1 Avoidance*

This option represents the decision not to undertake, when practicable, the activity that contains an intolerable risk. It means that management will choose an alternative that is either a different more tolerable approach to completing the required activity or different and less risky methodology or process within the activity.

There is the option of adopting an alternative work practice of lower risk that may reduce the consequences and/or likelihood of harm or loss but this would not necessarily be avoidance of risk. Avoiding the risk is equivalent to refusing to accept the risk e.g., transferring the risk to a third party, a different process utilizing different processes and procedures, etc.

### *7.1.2 Loss Prevention*

This technique aims at reducing the frequency of a particular loss.

For example we can reduce the probability of a fire hazard by adopting construction techniques with materials that have a high level of fire resistance (risk prevention). Another approach to loss prevention and therefore reduction of loss frequency arising from third-party liability on products is through the introduction of quality control systems. Still another consideration aimed at reducing work-related injuries is the adoption of technical devices that are designed to prevent hazardous actions by machine operators. Of course staff training, regularly updated safety and awareness programs are an integral part of any successful loss prevention program.

### 7.1.3 Loss Reduction

This technique aims at reducing the severity of loss. It is noted that severity minimization techniques come into play while the loss event is occurring. Examples are fire doors closing or the activation of a sprinkler or fire suppression system which prevent a fire from spreading in a building.

Before installing and activating any technical loss prevention system it is advisable to complete a cost/benefit analysis. It should be clearly quantifiable that the economic benefits stemming from such actions (reducing the potential impact of a loss) are favorable. Convenience is reached only when the economic benefit is greater than the cost of risk treatment actions.

### 7.1.4 Separation, Duplication, Diversification

Separation is a risk control technique that aims at "separating" and dispersing a particular asset or activity among different locations.

Duplication is based on backups, spares, or copies of critical property, information, or capabilities and keeps them in reserve.

Diversification typically spreads loss exposures over numerous projects, products, markets, or regions thereby reducing the impact of a loss on an organization from a loss at a single location (significant reduction of critical assets at any one location).

Again the aim of these techniques—especially separation—is to prevent the concentration of goods, people, or business in a single location, market, or individual project. These methods typically act on the severity of risk. It is obvious that if goods, business, or people are highly concentrated, the Maximum Probable Loss surges to a greater level.

Usually implementing a risk control method involving separation means physical separation e.g., geographically. This said separation can also involve temporal separation, which entails planning that aims at preventing that goods, people, or business are concentrated in the same location at the same time. For instance, by preventing several hazardous activities from being performed simultaneously or through the coordination of arrivals and departures of goods or people to and from the facility by providing a reasonable time gap between each phase of production will reduce the likelihood of a loss.

Risk control techniques should be selected and combined on the basis of a careful evaluation of costs and savings resulting from those decisions.

Costs and savings are broken down into direct and indirect costs and savings.

Direct costs resulting from the use of risk control techniques are in turn broken down into investment costs and operating costs. The former consist in the amount of capital required to purchase loss control equipment or modify subject machinery, plant, or buildings. The latter are basically costs incurred to implement

Table 7.1 Costs and savings of risk control techniques

| | Direct | Indirect |
|---|---|---|
| Costs | Investment costs for: | Reduced production: |
| | (a) purchase of control systems and devices | (a) temporary |
| | (b) facilities modification | (b) final |
| Savings/ benefits | Reduction of insurance costs | Risk abatement for non-insurable events |
| | Incentives for general investments | Risk abatement for uninsured events |
| | Incentives for investments in safety | Improvement in: |
| | | (a) productivity |
| | | (b) supply chain relationships |
| | | (c) public relations |

control devices and safety systems and keep them in good working order. Also to be considered are labor costs for fire-fighting and first aid teams and costs of regularly conducted safety training courses for the staff.

On the other hand, direct savings consist in the abatement of insurance costs as well as obtaining any government or local incentives for general investments or specific investments in safety and prevention.

Conversely, indirect costs include costs associated with production downtimes due to the time required to install control devices or systems or a reduction of production resulting from an ongoing interference by such control systems.

Finally, indirect savings include the savings associated with the abatement of the frequency and/or severity of a potentially detrimental event, due to the introduction of control measures. The indirect savings can be significant particularly for non-insurable events or those events which, albeit insurable, are only partially covered by insurance. Noteworthy among indirect savings are those that can be achieved by the improvement of the corporate image, industrial relations, and public relations (see Table 7.1).

## 7.2 Risk Financing

Risk financing represents a set of acts and decisions generating the funds to pay for losses or offset the volatility in cash flows that may occur from loss. Risk financing techniques are most commonly referred to as *retention* and *transfer*.

The strategic goal of risk financing techniques is to maintain the appropriate level of liquidity, managing the uncertainty resulting from loss outcome, and hence managing the total cost of risk. Another strategic goal of Risk Financing is to be compliant with legal requirements (Haimes 1998, Harrington 1999, Rothschild and Stiglitz 1976).

## 7.3 Risk Financing: Retention

This technique aims at absorbing the loss by generating funds within the organization to pay for the loss.

Retention can be represented as the voluntary or active assumption of a loss exposure that has been identified and analyzed (planned retention). In these cases, this planned retention is chosen for the purpose of cost-effectiveness or convenience.

In other cases, there could be an unplanned retention, which is the inadvertent or passive assumption of a loss and its consequence, either direct or indirect, because the loss exposure had not been identified or accurately analyzed.

### *7.3.1 Retention: Take a Proper Decision!*

Active risk retention is generally linked to at least one of the following conditions:

1. Impossibility to transfer or eliminate risk. This may occur, for instance, when no insurer accepts to insure the risk, while its elimination would entail winding up the business.
2. Excessive transfer costs. This may occur if the frequency and/or severity of the event, as calculated by the insurer are significantly higher than that reasonably expected by the company based on past experiences and therefore the relevant premium is deemed too high. Alternatively, one may find the insurer is prepared to take on the risk but only subject to certain prevention and/or abatement measures being implemented. These measures can be quite costly and may be deemed to be too high.
3. Very low probability of the event occurring, to the extent of being assumed in its totality.
4. Very high probability of the event occurring. In this case it is obvious that, in the presence of an essentially certain event, an insurer, albeit prepared to take on the risk, would demand a premium at least equal to, but often higher than, the Maximum Probable Loss.
5. Highly reliable risk measurement. This situation may arise only when the company holds the control over a large number of consistent and independent risk units, so that its forecasting capacity is highly effective.

The existence of one of the conditions listed above is a necessary, albeit not uniquely sufficient, condition for retention to be recommended as a risk treatment technique. Indeed, further factors need to be carefully considered before making final decisions regarding retention, including:

1. Savings on operating costs and insurer's profits. Risk retention rather than insurance transfer has the advantage of saving on the mark-up that the insurer must add to the pure premium to cover their acquisition (commissions and

**Table 7.2** Evaluation of the alternative between retention or transfer

| Retention or transfer? | |
|---|---|
| **Necessary conditions** | **Costs and savings** |
| Impossibility to transfer or eliminate risk | Savings from premium mark-up |
| Excessive transfer costs | Differential savings from the rate of external and in-house corporate premium |
| | Disbursement actualization for premiums and temporal sequence of losses |
| Very low probability event | Influence of taxation |
| Very high probability event | Additional loss management costs |
| High reliability in measuring risk | |

general sales expenses) and management costs as well as profits related to the assumption of the risk.

2. The savings between the loss expected by the insurer and the loss measured by the company. This occurs whenever the pure premium rate as calculated by the insurer exceeds the premium expected by the company based on past experiences.
3. The financial effect associated with the different time sequence of insurance premium payments compared to the losses projected to occur in the future.
4. The effect on taxation. The retention choice creates consequences on the yearly amount of income tax payable that are not easily foreseeable. Indeed, unlike insurance transfer whose cost, which is equal to the premium paid and is a tax deduction, tends to be evenly distributed over time, the losses incurred with the retention, albeit tax deductible, may not be as regular. This makes tax planning quite difficult.
5. Additional loss management costs. The retention of certain risk categories (especially third-party liability or workers compensation risks) requires the company to implement and manage a broad range of operations and services, including claim handling. This will entail the creation of a structure which, albeit on a smaller scale, reflects the structure of the typical insurance company. This will result in a series of ongoing costs to be considered at the time the decision is made.

The factors to be considered at the time of assessing the alternative between retention and insurance transfer are summarized in Table 7.2.

Therefore, retention is linked to a careful financial planning in order to control future losses. It is essential that the following factors can be taken into account:

- Ability to estimate costs with reasonable reliability. Indeed, when risks are treated by way of insurance transfer their cost can be easily determined as it is expressed by the premium paid. Conversely, when they are retained, there is the danger that they are not as easily assessed.

- Stabilization of economic results. The lack of financial planning for losses would make economic results highly volatile, as they would be linked to the occurrence or otherwise of unfavorable events. This volatility can, in turn, result in damaging consequences.
- Minimization of business interruption. The arrangement of ways to finance losses for retained risks is also required by the need to restrict, as much as possible, business interruption. Where this is lacking, the need to put in place impromptu intervention creates the premise for a possible delay in implementing recovery operations.

The methods that can be adopted to finance retention programs are many, and below we shall describe what can be considered best practice in this regard.

### 7.3.2 Asset Reduction

While considered an atypical way of financing retained risks, as it simply consists in accepting the asset reduction caused by the occurrence of the event even if this means winding up the business or a particular production line. Although at first glance it may seem simplistic, this method, if the result of a proper consideration of the situation is an effective means of retention. For example, whenever the cost for repairing or replacing the destroyed or damaged asset is so high as to make the continuation of production anti-economical. It is also possible to choose insurance transfer based on the replacement cost for the asset rather than its current value: however, this choice entails a significant hike in the premium, which may be considered excessive in relation to the cost effectiveness of the management.

Therefore, a choice could be made not to set aside resources to finance losses linked to risk retention when:

- the cost to repair or replace the asset is deemed greater than the profitability that can be expected from it;
- the total or partial loss of the asset does not affect in a material way the continuation of the business, i.e. when its contribution to the company's profitability is nil or close to nil.

### 7.3.3 Absorption into the Operating Costs

A relatively simple method of financing risks, in relation to which retention has been adopted, is to take into account predicted losses at the time of the financial planning of operations. In other words, when we develop operational budgets, these will need to include the forecast of costs for losses arising from retained events.

This choice is strictly linked to the degree of sophistication and success in predicting losses. This restricts the use of such a technique essentially to events which are prone to create frequent and small losses. In these cases, as properly observed, in addition to the general advantages of retention there is the advantage of bringing such costs under the control of cost center managers in the same way as any other operational expense for the business.

### *7.3.4 Self-insurance (Self-insured Retention)*

The financing of losses through their prediction and absorption into operating costs is feasible provided the events meet all the criteria of predictability and manageability. As mentioned previously these are usually loss that are predicability frequent but small. In case of events that are prone to less predictability and wider fluctuations in value the alternative to insurance transfer requires that the company become, on a small scale, an insurer. Seen under this light, self-insurance may be described as a financial plan whereby through yearly allocations the company creates a fund which, managed with more or less the same criteria applied by an insurer, allows the handling of losses as they fluctuate.

In addition to the above, further benefits that may be derived from self-insurance are:

- a strong incentive to perform in a more efficient manner the business typical of an insurer for its own account;
- the greater flexibility made possible by a self-insurance plan in treating risk, in the sense that insurance contracts often contain restrictive clauses for the insured;
- the improvement of physical control activities resulting from an in-house plan and where the use of an external insurer may amount to a disincentive;
- the improvement of claim payouts when losses do occur. As there are no conflicts of interest the time required to recover the losses, compared to the claim payout process of a normal insurer, are significantly reduced.

While there are many potential benefits the adoption of a self-insurance plan also has a range of limitations that should be considered when making a decision. Such limitations include:

- an insufficient number of consistent and independent risk units. In this case, the loss prediction is unreliable and in turn results in errors in calculating the yearly allocations;
- inefficiencies in managing the self-insurance plan also linked to inexperience compared to a third-party insurance company.

The difficulty in predicating tax deductibility of the yearly allocations and the subsequent effects on annual tax planning.

### *7.3.5 How Should Reserves be Allocated?*

An issue that emerges in all self-insurance plans concerns the allocation of yearly reserves: i.e., whether they should be linked or otherwise connected to investments in assets which can be readily disposed of.

Obviously, it is necessary, when developing a financial plan, to predict the maintenance of the overall liquidity situation which is also compatible with the requirements of the self-insurance plan.

This means that the reserve to be allocated yearly should be greater than the mere distribution of losses expected in the long term and therefore will have a dual component: (a) capital invested to cover atypical fluctuations; (b) yearly premium relating to a medium expected loss.

A general and relatively simplified method to determine the size of the reserve to be allocated and assess the choice between insurance transfer and self-insurance is the comparison between the company's financial situation at the beginning and the end of the financial year, both when resorting to insurance transfer and when adopting a self-insurance plan.

The final financial position, in case of insurance transfer, is equal to the initial net capital less the insurance premium to be paid plus the company's in-house profitability on the residual invested capital, according to the following formula:

$$\text{FPwi} = \text{iNC} - \text{IF} + r(\text{iCN} - \text{FPwi})$$

where FPwi = final position with insurance; iNC = initial net capital; IF = insurance fee; $r$ = in-house company's profitability rate.

Where a self-insurance plan is chosen, the final position will be equal to the initial net capital less the medium loss expected for the year plus the company's in-house profitability on the residual invested capital (less the reserves allocated for self-insurance) and further increased by the profitability resulting from the investment of the self-insurance reserves, according to the following formula:

$$\text{FPwsi} = \text{iCN} - \text{L}/2 - + - r(\text{iCN} - \text{L}/2 - R) + \text{i}R$$

where FPwai = final position with self-insurance; L/2 = medium expected loss; $R$ = reserves allocated as per the self-insurance plan; i = profitability rate resulting from the investment of the funds.

According to this model we should resort to insurance transfer whenever

$$\text{FPwi} > \text{FPwsi}.$$

A further simplification of the model may be achieved by indicating with $D$ the difference between the two final positions (with insurance and self-insurance), i.e.

$$D = \text{FPwi} - \text{FPwsi}.$$

If this formula is used, insurance transfer should be chosen whenever $D$ has positive values.

In considering this model (that however does not take into account the effects of taxation) it should be stressed that it is based on the provision that the funds allocated are invested in assets that can easily be disposed of and that the yield from such financial investments is in any case lower than the in-house company profitability rate. This is not always in all cases a realistic scenario.

### *7.3.6 Reserve Funds*

Another method of financing losses resulting from retained risks is the use of generic reserve funds, to be used when the event occurs. Unlike self-insurance, in this case there does not exist an accurate and strict yearly reserve appropriation plan based on the distribution of the losses of the risk being considered. Every year, especially in the years with favorable economic results, and irrespective of the size of the predicted losses, generic and indistinct reserves are allocated.

The use of reserve funds as a method for ensuring the financial control of losses has at least three contra indications:

1. In the year in which the loss has occurred and the reserve funds have been used wholly or partially to cover it, there is the concrete danger of not having such reserves available for alternative investment opportunities that were to arise unexpectedly.
2. Major problems may arise in the company liquidity. If, indeed, the reserves have been invested in assets that are marginally liquid or that are hard to dispose of, should a loss causing event occur, there will be the need to sell in a short period of time nonliquid assets in order to handle the unexpected situation. This may result in capital losses at the time of their disposal.
3. The resulting loss may be so serious and significant that the available resources in the form of reserves may not be sufficient to cover the loss and to continue the company business.

### *7.3.7 Contingent Credit Lines*

An alternative and to some extent innovative way of providing financial control over the losses is the establishment of contingent credit lines to be used only when the loss does occur.

Resorting to this method, as an alternative, for example, to insurance transfer, may be justified by a gap, which has occurred in recent years, between the percentile increments of the insurance premiums in many sectors and the trend of the cost of money. In some cases we have seen that the financing of losses through contingent capital may be less-expensive than the payment of an insurance premium over many years.

Organizations usually select a partial retention, regarding only a portion of the cost of any loss, instead of retaining the full cost of any loss. The capability to select properly the portion and nature of costs to be retained represent a key driver for an effective balance between retention and transfer.

## 7.4 Risk Financing: Transfer

Transfer comprehends insurance and non-insurance techniques that transfer the financial consequences of certain specified loss to another party.

*Insurance* is a risk financing technique that transfers the potential financial consequences of a certain specified loss from the insured to the insurer.

The goal is to transfer risks to a large group which agrees to share the financial losses in exchange for premium payments. The purpose of insurance is to spread the hazard risk among many who have similar risks.

The typical insurable risk is a pure risk, measurable and definite in terms of time, cause, and location, typically accidental, unintended, and unintentional.

Moreover, an insurable risk should be:

- homogenous, meaning similar, if losses are similar it means that they respond to similar causes of loss, this will improve predictability;
- independent and not catastrophic, meaning that only a small percentage of insureds will face a loss at any one time, so the premium of the many will pay the loss of the few unfortunate. Losses should not be catastrophic otherwise the financial stability of the insurer will be seriously challenged;
- affordable, meaning that the insurance makes good economic sense to purchase it.

*Noninsurance* is a risk financing technique that transfers all or part of the financial loss consequences to another party, other than an insurer.

Typically, there are two methods:

1. transfer through the abandonment or sale of an asset: in this case the risk is permanently transferred along with the asset;
2. contractual transfer: a risk, quite often the third-party liability risk, is transferred to a counterparty in the relevant contract.

Contractual transfer is a risk financing technique whose aim is to create such conditions so that upon the unfavorable event occurring, the company may have legal recourse against a third party to cover the losses incurred. The two main cases are recoupment and bonds/security.

Contractual transfer may take place by either a negative transfer, i.e., striking out existing clauses which make the company responsible for the consequences of the risk, or a positive transfer, i.e., by inserting clauses that penalize the other party. Examples of contractual transfer in sale contracts are the mercantile clauses such as "ex works" or, in case of ocean cargo "fob" (free on board) when dealing with customers and "free at destination" when dealing with suppliers. Or, when dealing with one's own customers, by inserting clauses that aim at ruling out any company's third-party liability for any damage resulting from the use of the product.

The transfer techniques for abandonment should be kept separate from those for avoidance and elimination because they do not alter the frequency and severity of the unfavorable event, which continues to exist, albeit borne by others.

Among the typical types of insurance there are:

1. Property
2. Business income
3. General Liability
4. Workers' compensation and employers' liability
5. Motor vehicle
6. Employers' liability
7. Flood
8. Directors' and officers' liability.

### 7.4.1 Property

First-party insurance indemnifies the owner or user of property for its loss, or the loss of its income-producing ability, when the loss or damage is caused by a covered peril, such as fire or explosion. Accordingly, property insurance encompasses inland marine, boiler and machinery, and crime insurance, as well as what was once known as fire insurance, now simply called property insurance: insurance on buildings and their contents.

A commercial property policy consists of: one or more coverage forms; one or more causes of loss forms; the commercial property conditions form; and the common policy conditions form. The most widely used commercial property coverage forms are the building and personal property coverage form and the business income and extra expense coverage form.

In the "Named Perils form", the property insurance term refers to policies that provide coverage only for loss caused by the perils specifically listed as covered. It contrasts with all risks coverage, which applies to loss from all causes not specifically listed as excluded.

Coverage is provided against perils like fire, lightning, explosion, smoke, windstorm, hail, riot, civil commotion, aircraft, vehicles, vandalism, sprinkler leakage, sinkhole collapse, and volcanic action.

In the broad form, coverage is ensured against additional perils, like falling objects; weight of snow, ice, or sleet; water damage (in the form of leakage from appliances); and collapse due to specified causes.

In the "All risk form", property insurance covering losses arising from any fortuitous cause except those that are specifically excluded. This is in contrast with named perils coverage which applies only to loss arising from causes that are listed as covered.

A particularly crucial issue when dealing with insurance transfer of the risk is the setting of the value of the insured assets. This because, as is well-known, in calculating the compensation, the so-called proportional rule is applied, whereby the compensation is equal to the damage multiplied by a coefficient resulting from the ratio between the insured value of the asset and its actual value at the time of the damage, i.e.,

$$I = \mathrm{VA}/\mathrm{VE}.\ \mathrm{D} \quad (\text{compensation} = \text{insured value}/\text{actual value}/\text{damage})$$

where $I$ = compensation; VA = insured value; VE = actual value; D = damage.

According to the general conditions, once the damage has occurred, the actual value is determined based on the restoration cost net of depreciation (taking into account age, state of maintenance, building technique, location, destination, and so forth). However, it is possible to waive such assessment criteria by putting a "new for old" clause in, whereby the actual value is calculated without deducting depreciation. It is also possible to obtain compensation based on the replacement cost at the time of the loss (subject to an additional premium).

The use of the proportional rule upon the disposal of the asset may be an extra reason why the company places special focus on ensuring that the insured values are very close to the actual values and are continuously updated. The issue of a different assessment of the assets before and after the accident may be overcome by resorting to the so-called preventive estimation. This estimation, to be performed by a party independent to both the insured and the insurer and accepted by both parties, allows for the elimination of the proportional rule. The cost of the estimation, which can be quite high, is borne by the insured and the estimation should be performed on a regular basis e.g., annually or bi-annually.

### *7.4.2 Business Income*

Business income insurance is usually included within the property insurance policy and covers loss of income, suffered by a business, when damage to its premises, equipment, or contents by a covered cause of loss, causes a slowdown or

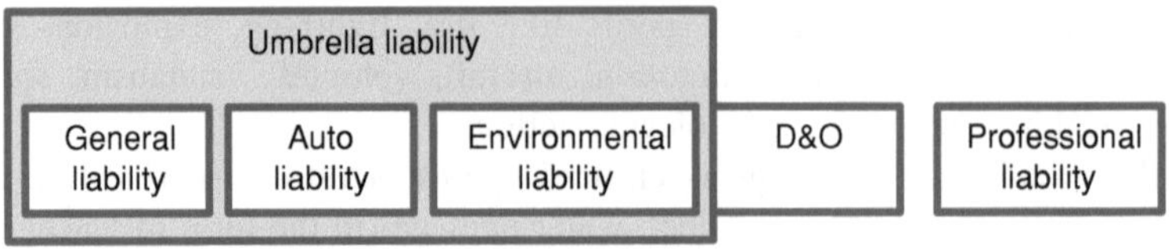


**Fig. 7.2** The insurance liability

suspension of its operations during the time required to repair or replace the damaged property, equipment, and contents.

There are two business income coverage forms:

- the business income and extra expense coverage form;
- or the business income coverage form without extra expense.

## *7.4.3 General Liability*

General liability or third-party liability insurance protects a commercial insured from most liability exposures other than motor vehicle and professional liability.

### 7.4.3.1 Commercial General Liability

This is a standard insurance policy issued to business organizations to protect them against liability claims for bodily injury and property damage arising from premises, operations, products, and completed operations and personal injury liability.

### 7.4.3.2 Umbrella Liability

This is a policy designed to provide protection against catastrophic losses. It is generally written to provide higher limits over the various primary liability policies including business motor vehicle policy, commercial general liability (CGL) policy, watercraft and aircraft liability policies, and employers' liability coverage. The umbrella policy has three purposes: it provides excess limits when the limits of underlying liability policies are exhausted by the payment of claims; it drops down and picks up where the underlying policy leaves off when the aggregate limit of the underlying policy in question is exhausted by the payment of claims; and it provides protection against some claims not covered by the underlying policies, subject to the assumption, by the named insured, of a self-insured retention (Fig. 7.2).

This insurance coverage is effective for providing additional limits above the per-occurrence limits of the insured's underlying liability coverage. This "umbrella" can be adopted for the purpose of covering some losses that the underlying insurance does not cover and can take place when the underlying aggregate limits are exhausted.

### *7.4.4 Workers' Compensation*

The Workers' Compensation Insurance policy provides indemnification and rehabilitation expenses to an employee for a work-related injury (including fatalities).

### *7.4.5 Motor Vehicle Liability*

This insurance policy will cover bodily injury and property damage that the policy holder causes while operating a vehicle.

### *7.4.6 Employers' Liability*

This coverage provided by this policy is typically provided by endorsement to the basic workers' compensation policy and pays on behalf of the insured (employer) all sums that the insured shall become legally obligated to pay as damages because of bodily injury by accident or disease suffered by any employee of the insured arising from and during his employment by the insured.

### *7.4.7 Flood*

Provides coverage for damage to property caused by flood. It may be available either as standalone coverage or as an endorsement to almost any property insurance policy. Normally, the coverage provided is subject to a per occurrence sub-limit, an annual aggregate limit, and a separate deductible.

### *7.4.8 Directors' and Officers' Liability*

This coverage operates for corporate Directors and Officers (D&O) against claims, very often by stockholders and employees, alleging financial loss arising from mismanagement. D&O forms are written on a claims-made basis, generally contain no explicit duty to defend the insured, and exclude intentional/dishonest acts and bodily injury and property damage.

### 7.4.9 Take Care in Evaluating the Insurance Cost!

The criteria affecting the level of funding for treating risks should be established at the outset of the risk management process as part of the strategic, organizational, and risk management.

The strategic goal is to find an effective and efficient combination of actions that allow the organization to proactively face Risks, controlling the Total Cost of Risk.

For these reasons the true cost of insurance needs to be considered very carefully.

The yearly insurance spend should be compared with the median expected loss as determined when calculating the risk. If, based on early approximation, the values thus achieved seem similar, the cost of the insurance transfer would be nil.

We should not forget, however, that to the insurance fee we need to add the costs covering the additional services provided by the insurer, such as claim payouts or any insurance consultancy fees for physically controlling the risk.

Of course, an in-depth examination of this comparison requires the consideration of the distribution of losses over time, especially as regards their extent. If this is possible, the comparison should be made between the value of the losses and the value of the premiums paid annually in advance.

As regards the limitations pertaining to the insurance transfer, they may be summarized as follows:

1. Not all risks can be insured. The features whereby a risk may be transferred to an insurer are: (a) the existence of a large enough number of quite consistent and independent units exposed to risk; (b) the event should be accidental and fortuitous both for the insured and the insurer; (c) each loss must be able to be quantifiable as far as time, place, cause, and amount are concerned and must be able to be measured in monetary terms; (d) the expected loss should be large enough to justify the insurance costs.
2. On those occasions, when an insurer provides a full and total compensation for losses incurred, especially indirect losses the claim payout process requires times and typically the methods do not allow for an immediate return to the status that existed prior to the loss. These ramifications should always be kept in mind by the insured.
3. Not all premiums are certain. There are some types of insurances for which the premium is conventionally set on the basis of certain measures that are subjected to change during the insurance period. For example, the size of stocks or the amount of the employee remuneration for third-party liability. As a result,

**Table 7.3** Benefits and costs of the captive insurance company

| Benefits of the captive insurance company | Costs of the captive insurance company |
|---|---|
| 1. Abatement of insurance costs | 1. Incorporation and operating costs |
| 2. Access to reinsurance market | 2. Capital lockup |
| 3. Improvement of the corporate cash flows | 3. Risk of unfavorable results |
| 4. Profitability | 4. Innocent capacity |
| 5. Effects on taxation | 5. Reduced focus on physical controls over the risk |
| 6. Instrumental in the insurance negotiations | |
| 7. Transfer of uninsurable risks | |
| 8. Development of an independent insurance business | |

in these cases the total premium may be unknown when the decision to transfer the risk or otherwise needs to be made.

In addition to the limitations described above, we should consider a further and perhaps just as important is the limitation of the legal contents of a contract whereby the risk is transferred to the insurer. There has been a trend to consolidate basic contracts and exclusion clauses (mainly in favor of the insurer) that at times limit the efficacy of the contract.

### 7.4.10 What is a Captive Insurance Company?

In dealing with self-insurance we highlighted how one of the main drawbacks of its use is the fact that the yearly allocations provided for in the program are not always or completely tax deductible in addition there can be timing issues for tax deductibility. An option is to create a captive insurance company, i.e. a legally independent company owned insurer to which its own risks may be contractually transferred for a consideration.

In order to assess the convenience to establish a captive insurance company, several factors need to be considered (see Table 7.3).

An immediate advantage is the abatement of a portion of the insurance costs due to the savings of the premium mark-up charged by a normal insurer (acquisition costs, part of the operating costs, taxes on premiums, and so forth).

Another and just as important advantage is the possibility of directly accessing the reinsurance market which, being made up of insurers who are different from those of the primary market, is often based on different approaches to risk, which in turn may lead to advantageous contractual opportunities.

The use of a captive insurer may results in a significant improvement of the corporate financial flows. Indeed, while with a traditional third-party insurance program the premium usually needs to be paid in advance, the payment of a portion of the premium to a captive insurance company may be delayed until the latter needs cash to pay out claims. Moreover, where the captive insurance company chooses to access the reinsurance market, the conventions of the latter often offered installment options for premium payment, thereby furnishing a further cash flow benefit. And if, as it often happens, the premiums for risk transfers are duly paid to the captive insurance company, a further benefit would ensue, consisting in the ability of retaining and using their profitability inside the group, which in future could generate further premium savings.

Along with the favorable factors, we should of course consider the costs associated with the establishment of such an owned entity. First, the incorporation and operating costs may be sizeable. Second, running a captive entity also requires significant professional skills. Third, we consider the fact that, as protection against the possible fluctuation of the losses arising out of the risks taken over, the captive insurance company must have an initial capital, which can be substantial depending on the risk and limits transferred to the captive which means locking up assets. For the parent company this initial capital amounts to tied capital and we cannot neglect the opportunity costs involved. We should also carefully assess the risk of unfavorable results, associated with either the occurrence of losses greater than those expected or the eventual lack of the protection achieved through the reinsurance.

A further factor to be considered is the fact that only in theory can risks not otherwise insurable also be transferred to the captive insurance company. Indeed it is not possible for any risk to be assigned only because this is done by a company controlled by the parent company, without any consideration for the long-term nature of the business it is called upon to perform.

## 7.5 Decision Making

Decision making is the cognitive process which leads to the selection of a set of actions among several alternative scenarios.

In risk management, decision making is not only about acting for eliminating risk. The goal is to protect the company from risks in an effective and efficient way. Hence, risk management decision making leads to the selection of those actions that can reduce and/or mitigate critical risks, assuring an economic benefit for the company.

It means that the cost of risk management actions implemented (like mitigations or transfer actions) should not exceed the saving that the company can get from the reduced risk profile.

Total costs of risk management actions should be assessed and selected with respect to time, operations, and human resources dedicated to risk assessment (administrative costs), comprehending risk control costs, risk financing costs, and the cost of both direct and indirect loss.

## 7.6 How to Measure the Cost of Risk?

The Cost of Risk (CoR) is a quantitative measurement of the costs of the negative events coming from risk occurrence compared with the costs related to risk management activities (risk control and risk financing).

In many organizations the CoR represents the budget that risk managers and insurance buyer should work with. This value comprehends the whole risk exposure, direct costs for risk treatment actions, financial results of captive insurance companies, costs related to the risk management function and all the fees, premiums, and commissions to brokers, insurer, and consultant as applicable.

From a strictly financial perspective the CoR measurement is typically expressed by the costs of managing risk through efficient use of capital (debt, equity, and off-balance sheet). The goal of an enterprise-wide analysis of the CoR is to understand and measure the investments and benefits related to:

- corporate risk profile;
- risk prevention strategies;
- better decision-making processes;
- improvements of process robustness;
- shareholder value and increased profitability.

The goal of the comparison is to determine whether the total costs of the risk management function are increasing, decreasing, or remaining constant as a function of the economic activity of the business. After the quantitative measurement has been derived, a comparison can be made between the CoR of that business and the CoRs of its peer groups. In addition, CoR will allow the business to focus on the areas of operation that will have the greatest long-term impact on its total risk management function costs.

Managers should accept reasonable risks and prepare contingency plans for the risks that pose the greatest threat to survival and success of the business.

## 7.7 External contribution 7.1: Innovation in the Context of Risk Management

Innovation in the context of risk management might seem somewhat out of place since we have said that enterprise risk management is all about mitigation and control of risk. Many will equate innovation with taking risk whether it can be incremental in relation to the existing products, services or methods of administration or disruptive in nature completely changing the product or service offering and how business is administrated.

But in order to better understand the role of innovation in the risk management process we can start by defining what we mean by innovation:

- enhanced features on existing products;
- replication of someone else's smart product;
- design of a brand new product;
- market movement of an existing product;
- geographic expansion.

Innovation actual takes many forms and in some cases it is the small movement on an existing product or service that can make all the difference. Continuous process improvement in the risk management processes and procedures will fall into the category of incremental innovation. Implementation of an advanced technological platform for modeling risks and the ability to assume more risk as an organization might be considered disruptive innovation.

In order to make innovation part of a successful enterprise risk management system there five ways to jump start the thinking required to embed innovative thinking the risk management process:

1. Go outside the comfort zone—seek the unpredictable.
2. Challenge the default position.
3. Try it!—testing and prototype. Fast failure is the key to fast success.
4. "What if that wasn't the question?"—challenge our assumptions.
5. Share all learning.

The "why be concerned" about innovation is tied to the organization's stakeholders. With the continuously evolving risks that an organization must manage it is critical to get "out in front". Innovation = anticipation. The more the organization can understanding the effects of this constantly changing risk landscape the better able they will be able to make risk management a competitive advantage. This is represented in Fig. 7.3.

What are the key attributes of an innovative organization and executive team:

- Visionary Executives and recognized thought leaders;
- strong risk appetite—"Fail, fail again, fail better." (S. Beckett);
- high profile of innovation internally—most staff engaged;
- continuous investment through cycles and some off cycle funding;
- repeatable formula and project management;
- innovation Champions—the viral distributors.

Innovation requires discipline and planning, one can say very much aligned with a successful enterprise risk management process.

Innovation in risk management cannot be completed in isolation it involves shared responsibility and hard work, so-called "collective intelligence". Other key factors in a disciplined approach to innovation in the context of enterprise risk management can be summed up as follows:

- comprehensive measurement and marketing;
- customer involvement and asymmetric 'peer' analysis—benchmarking is fine—as long as it is against interesting parallels, not industry leaders;

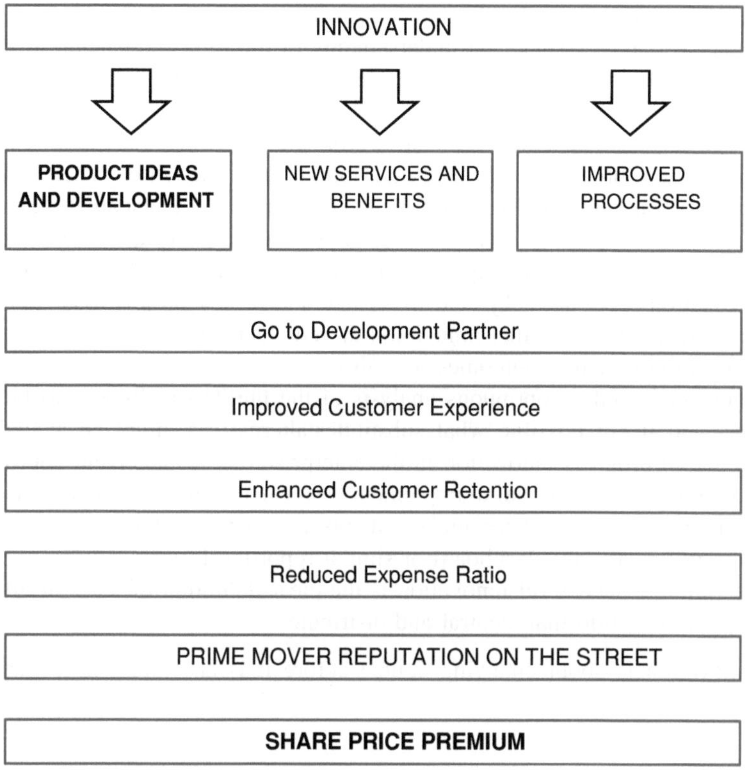


**Fig. 7.3** Innovative thinking and risk management process

- celebrate the success and the failures—employee recognition and lessons learned.

As Lou Gestner of IBM stated: "In the end management doesn't change culture. Management invites the workforce itself to change culture".

So how does management invite a workforce to become intelligent and innovative risk takers instead of passive risk assumers?

As mentioned previously the organization must start with a clearly defined innovation process. This process overlaid with a well articulated enterprise risk management approach will include:

- The innovation purpose—guidance on the objectives is essential to the proper alignment of new products, services, processes, and procedures. Without a clear line of sight in conjunction with the organization's strategic mission the innovation process is destined to fail.
- The success profile—in fact it is critical to envision what success would look like for the organization. Just as with the ERM process understanding the destination will be as important as taking the voyage.

- Size of benefits, timing, and sequencing—innovation comes in many sizes but whether it is big or small the understanding of the right sequencing to bring a process or procedure into action and become part of the organization's DNA has to be properly analyzed.
- The governance scheme—innovation for the sake of innovation can pull important resources away from critical organization activities. Therefore, it is critical to continuously check and report in an open and transparent manner the progress of the process in order to guarantee an ongoing alignment with the organization's overall strategy. As mentioned before so many aspects of an organization's life are subjected to change and proper project management in this context can assure that innovation driven change remains aligned with the organization's desired outcomes over time.
- Alignment includes continuous analysis of the hurdles/roadblocks to be overcome, and if not possible what substitutes/alternatives might be available to continue to progress innovation in the enterprise risk management approach.
- Once in place it is essential to implement performance measurement/metrics and reporting on results. These measurements may be presented in the form of milestones or a status dashboard or similar reporting format.
- Underpinning successful innovation is the clear definition of team in all of its forms: formal, informal, central and distributed.

"Innovation is about changing course before it is absolutely necessary" (T. Peters).

## *Author Profile*

Tony Cabot—Director Product Development for Europe and Asia—Argo Group
Senior Executive Officer—Argo Re (DIFC) Ltd.

Responsibilities as Director of Product Development for Europe and Asia role include providing a fluent and comprehensive system of Product Development that ensures that good ideas get to market in a controlled and consistent manner with minimal delay.

As the Senior Executive Officer for Argo Re DIFC Ltd. in Dubai, UAE Tony has responsibilities for setting the strategic direction of this subsidiary in alignment with the Argo group strategy in the MENA Region.

Tony is member of the CPCU Society's Board of Chapter Governors, International Insurance Interest Group and a founding member of the CPCU Society's Europe Chapter.

## 7.8 External contribution 7.2: The Role of an Insurance Partner

The role of an insurance partner is to provide coverage and risk management service either in the chosen line of business or in the chosen industry segments consistently on a medium to long-term basis.

In order to deploy the Partner's role an Insurance company should employee experts, and then maintain a constant level of investment in understanding the dynamics in the specific in the industry sectors chosen by the company.

In their role as Partner an Insurance company should help its clients with Loss Prevention advice, Business Continuity planning, Technical advices become a point of reference for its clients and able to opening share suggestions and remediation actions at 360°.

Like in the majority of European Insurance markets also in Italy the approach of Insurance companies is to be highly specialized in very few industry segments, such as Oil and Gas, Pharmaceutical, Aviations companies. This level specialization is driven by the treaty reinsurance market, and is strongly connected to the high volatility of some risks in these industries. This approach leaves all other industries to be insured with a standard approach, where most of the efforts are focused in adapting the policy wording to meet some needs.

An insurance company to become an Insurance Partner needs to put at the center of its organization the Customer to understand its operational risks along the value chain and potential liabilities and then to derive coverage and services needs. Insurance companies should help their customers becoming more competitive by avoiding risks which could impact the future strategic objectives set by the shareholders and damage their assets. Customers who have identified the risks associated with their activities and have chosen to manage these risks proactively have proven time and time again that in the moment of need they have survived and actually prosper further. A well known example was the loss at chip manufacturing plant of Philips in New Mexico in 2000. Nokia and Ericsson who, at that time, were competing head to head in the mobile manufacturing market were both supplied by this plant. Nokia knew about the risk and had in place a strong Business Continuity Plan; following the loss they contacted his alternative suppliers and kept Stakeholders informed. Ericsson instead was not so well organized. One year after the loss Ericsson shares lost approximately 40 % of their value while Nokia shares increased by almost 30 % and thanks to their brilliant organization they strengthened their market leadership in Mobile phones. Other more recent examples can be found following the March 2011 Earthquake loss in Tohoku region in Japan as mentioned in the Global Risks 2012 survey commissioned by the World Economic Forum. Lawson a Japanese convenience store chain thanks to their Business Continuity Management recovered within 4 days from the Earthquake its production lines and logistics hub sufficiently to resume approximately 80 % of its business.

RSA are one of the world's leading renewable energy insurers, with an in-depth understanding of the renewable energy industry built up through working with some of the biggest and most innovative clients in the sector.

For over 20 years our expertise and global reach delivers protection at every stage of development, from planning and transportation through to construction and operation. Effective insurance and risk management is required to protect these investments and help ensure that the renewables industry continues to develop at pace.

We provide insurance covers across the full customer experience including from the early shipment of material, through the construction phase and providing Property, Business Interruption, Liability, Engineering and Marine coverage during the operational life of the facilities, to Loss Prevention advise to help RSA customers to mitigate the consequences of negative events. We provide insurance covers for a wide range of renewable energy technologies including:

- Wind Energy—onshore and offshore facilities;
- Solar Energy—Photovoltaic, Concentrated and Thermal installations;
- Small Hydro—Power stations producing an output up to 50 MW;
- Bioenergy—Biomass, Biogas and Waste to Energy plants.

We offer specialized insurance solutions to a broad spectrum of clients and business partners including: Manufacturers, Utility companies, Independent power producers, Contractors, Investors.

Our Renewable Energy team, created in 2007, brings together the largest team of renewable energy insurance experts in the world with over 70 people in the team worldwide.

We are a market leader in the sector with around 10 % market share and have areas of clear market leadership such as offshore wind where we have an involvement in around 80 % of all offshore wind parks.

Our global operations are backed up and supported by three Centers of Excellence, that provide the best experts in the market place, who can be called upon when required:

- Canada—Hydro;
- UK—Solar and Biomass;
- Denmark—Wind.

## *Corporate Profile*

RSA, founded in 1710, are one of the world's leading multinational insurance groups. We can offer insurance solutions in over 150 countries and have leading or significant market positions in the UK, Scandinavia, and Canada. Our capacity is among the biggest and most secure in the marketplace. We have some 20 million customers around the globe and approximately 22,000 employees. In addition, we are a member of the Dow Jones Sustainability Index and the FTSE4 Good Index, and signatory to the United Nations Principles for Sustainable Insurance launched in RIO+20.

## References

Dionne G (2000) Handbook of insurance. Kluwer Academic Publishers Group, Boston

Haefeli D, Liedtke PM (2012) Insurance and resolution in light of the systemic risk debate: a contribution to the financial stability discussion in insurance. The Geneva Association, Geneva. www.genevaassociation.org

Haimes YY (1998) Risk modeling, assessment and management. Wiley, New York

Harrington SE (1999) Risk management and insurance. Irwin/McGraw-Hill, Boston

Rothschild M, Stiglitz J (1976) Equilibrium in competitive insurance markets: an essay on the economics of imperfect information. Q J Econ 90(4):629–649

## References

# Part IV
# Supply Chain Risk Management and Business Continuity

# Chapter 8
# Operational Risk and Supply Chain Risk Management

As described in the previous chapters, risks have been typically divided into four groups, which are strategic, financial, hazard, and *operational* risks.

The consideration of the central role of business processes and the relevance of their effective and efficient management have led us to present operational risk and supply chain risk as explicit topic of this handbook.

Risk management is the process devoted to protecting the organization and augmenting its capability to achieve its stated strategic objectives. Operational processes represent the core business of most companies, and therefore the proper assessment of operational and supply chain risks is critical to effective and efficient prevention and protection of an organization. In fact, the successful assessment of these risks can represent an important competitive advantage for the organization.

## 8.1 What is Operational Risk?

As a starting point, we define operational risk as the risk associated with the execution of a company's business functions. As Porter highlighted in 1996 "the essence of strategy is in the activities".

Taking this perspective, all the managers should be aware that activities, functions, and processes impact functional performance, business units' performance, and corporate performance and hence may generate risks that may impact both strategic and functional objectives.

According to this approach, all the methods and techniques devoted to manage operational risks should include proper consideration of their "strategic", "financial", and "functional" impacts (Holfmann 2010).

For example, as highlighted in previous chapters, higher cash flows are often associated with well managed business risk. When organizations are operating in stable environment, or when they are able to cope with uncertainty, corporate operations are more efficient and earnings volatility is lower. Moreover, there exist a positive correlation between the rate of return and the management of operational risk.

A. Borghesi and B. Gaudenzi, *Risk Management*, Perspectives in Business Culture, DOI: 10.1007/978-88-470-2531-8_8, © Springer-Verlag Italia 2013 

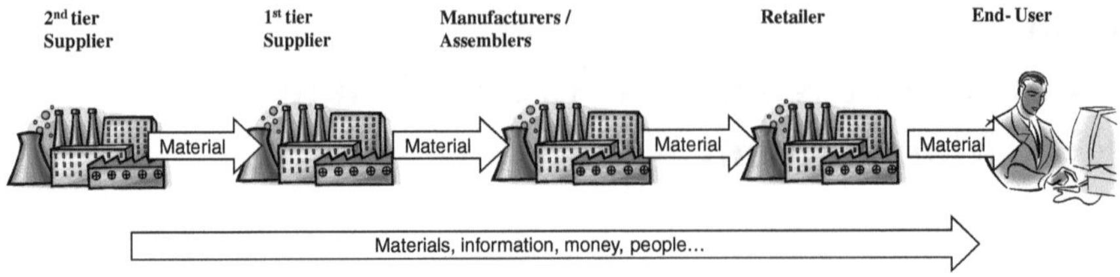


**Fig. 8.1** Actors along the supply chain

### *8.1.1 ... and Supply Chain Risk?*

In evaluating operations and business processes of an organization, the inter-organizational dimension should be carefully considered.

Supply chain risks are all risks related to the network's nature, strategies, and activities. A network is composed by *structural elements* (key actors involved, complexity of relationships among them, nature of goals, and climate of relationships in terms of collaboration and/or conflict) and *dynamic components* (human resources, products, projects, and know-how involved along these networks). All of these elements should be assessed as potential sources of risks.

## 8.2 Logistics and Supply Chain Management

In order to fully understand the scope and context of supply chain risk management a brief description of the concepts of logistics and supply chain is hereby provided.

In general, *logistics* are considered as the management of the flow of goods, information, money, and people between the point of origin and the point of destination in order to meet the requirements of customers or corporations. Logistics involve different actors and activities (see Fig. 8.1) like warehousing, inventory, transportation, integration with service provider (like 3PL or 4PL), material handling, packaging, security, and information sharing (Bowersox et al. 1995).

The *supply chain* has been defined as "…the network of organizations that are linked through upstream and downstream linkages, in the different processes and activities that produce value in the form of products and services in the hands of the ultimate customer" (Christopher 1998).

Researchers and practitioners have categorized supply chain processes in many different ways. Croxton et al. (2001) identified eight key processes which represent the core elements of supply chain management:

- customer relationship management;
- customer service management;

- demand management;
- order fulfillment;
- manufacturing flow management;
- procurement;
- product development and commercialization;
- returns management.

These processes run the length of the supply chain and cut across firms and "functional silos" within each firm. Functional silos are, for example marketing, finance, production, purchasing, and are typically managed in the perspective of the single organization, while the essential role of processes is that they cross the supply chain and have strategic and operational effects over the entire network.

Along a supply chain, all the actors should share common supply chain objectives with respect to the end user, which can be summarized into the goals of customer service and flexibility.

In managing supply chain risks, the nature of the strategic objectives should be considered in order to identify the potential sources of uncertainty and vulnerability.

### *8.2.1 The Goal of Customer Service*

The organizations within the supply chain typically aim to achieve the highest level of service for the customer, which is measurable in terms of the capability to deliver the right quantities, to the right places, at the right time, and in a cost-effective manner.

This objective can be measured, for example through the "perfect order-index", which evaluates the service performance in terms of on-time-delivery (the number of deliveries that meet customer expectations in terms of time), order completeness (the number of deliveries that are complete), and the percentage of damages and defects in delivered orders (the number of deliveries that have no defects/damages).

### *8.2.2 The Goal of Flexibility*

Competition rules are changing. Despite their dimension and sectors, companies are facing a more variable and unpredictable demand, global markets, products' complexity, and shorter lead times. In order to adapt to these rapid changes and criticalities, supply chains must be flexible enough to cope with the complexity and vulnerability.

In fact, it is the critical to managing risks along the supply chain that the level of complexity and vulnerability of these processes be carefully evaluated.

*Complexity* is a multi-faceted phenomenon. Production processes are complex due to the myriad of actors and business-to-business relationships which make the supply chain more complex. Add to this, the increasingly high level of customer expectation and the often multi-tiered supplier base; factors that also increase the vulnerability of the supply chain.

*Vulnerability* can be defined as the entire exposure to serious disturbance, arising from risks within the supply chain and outside, in the environment.

In particular, it is noted that the biggest risks may typically lie outside the company in the wider supply chain. Moreover, most of the critical risks are outside our control and the complexity of modern supply chains increases their vulnerability to disruption.

A report published by the Economist Intelligence Unit in 2011 highlighted that the most critical threats for next 3 years (listed in order of importance) are:

- insolvency of partners;
- labor disputes;
- IT failures;
- natural disasters;
- energy supply problems or price increase;
- protectionism measures;
- supply shortages;
- political instability;
- piracy and thefts.

Risks are therefore heterogeneous and their management requires the capability to consider simultaneously the correlations among different risk sources and supply chain actors.

## 8.3 Creating Resilient—and Less Vulnerable—Processes and Supply Chains

As Christopher stated (2004), a resilient supply chain can be defined as "a supply chain with the ability to recover quickly from unexpected events impacting supply chain performance".

The necessary steps in order to make a (more) resilient and less vulnerable supply chain are:

(a) Identifying key actors in the supply chain.
    Identifying the key actors—like unique suppliers, service providers, producers, and distributors—represent the first steps for an effective supply chain mapping (Gardner 2003).
    All of these actors should be addressed in terms of their criticality and dependency, and the quality of products/services provided. Hence, key relationships with the most critical actors should be managed with particular attention. Supply chain management must combine the capability to reduce

lead times and to achieve pipeline efficiency with key providers/actors. This requires the ability to interact and synchronize flows and information efficiently and effectively up and down the chain of the key providers/actors.

(b) Formalize supply chain risk management.
Supply chain risk has been defined as "any risk to information, material and product flow from original suppliers to the delivery of the final product" (Christopher 2003). Supply chain risks should be properly identified and managed by following some key steps (Jüttner et al. 2003):

- assessing the risk sources for the supply chain, like for example the functions of procurement, production, warehousing, R&D, transport and distribution;
- defining the potential adverse consequences and risk drivers on the supply chain, which means the risks to be identified and measured in each source;
- treating risks on the supply chain, on the basis of the global risk exposition, the amount of the budget available and the level of risk tolerance (for single risks and for the entire portfolio).

Risk drivers can be considered in terms of what generates risk; where the risk is; and what the risk is associated with. These factors can be identified in various ways and with different techniques, depending on the industrial sector, the risk management culture, the tolerance, and appetite to risks. However, supply chain risk assessment should be linked to the specific objectives of the supply chain which should "guide" the selection of risks to be measured (Gaudenzi and Borghesi 2006).

Supply chain risks are typically related to phenomenon connected with inventory and stock, like overstocking or stock outs (lost sales), quality, reliability, products/technology's obsolescence, availability of components and materials, and errors in forecasting and/or demand planning.

A globally recognized classification of supply chain risks is provided here below, with a succinct list of the associated risk drivers:

- supplier risks;
- process risks;
- market risks;
- environmental risks.

*Supplier risks* are typically related to the following risk drivers, which should be assessed and controlled systematically: dependency on key suppliers, lack of information in supply markets, quality, and management issues arising from offshore sourcing, potential disruption at 1st and 2nd tier level, length, and variability of replenishment lead times.

*Process risks* are for example: manufacturing yield variability, lengthy set-up times and inflexible processes, equipment reliability, limited capacity/bottlenecks, and outsourcing of key business processes.

*Market risks* are for example: loss of major accounts, volatility of demand, and concentration of customer base, short life cycles, and innovative competitors.

*Environmental risks* may be: natural disasters, terrorism and war, piracy and thefts, regulatory changes, duties and quotas, and strikes.

## *8.3.1 How to Assess Supply Chain Risks*

Looking at the body of the literature and practices, there are several approaches to risk assessment in the field of supply chain risk measurement.

Supply chain risks can be analyzed and evaluated in both qualitative and quantitative terms, particularly by using techniques that assign values to certain indicators for potential impacts and hence importance (Zsidisin 2004).

The quantitative evaluation of supply chain risk can be supported by statistical analysis, like the use of "failure modes and effect analysis" (FMEA) or Six Sigma, which investigate all of the events that may give rise to variations in process performance.

In a complex environment, statistical control tools can be helpful but these should be supported by qualitative tools, for two main reasons. First, in complex networks in which risk monitoring is a difficult challenge, it is worth looking for a transversal database of information. Second, from an operational and business risk perspective, statistical risk-modelling tools have been often identified as being "imperfect", because they could generate unfounded results when the models are not robust.

Decision making could thus become risky if it is based on a one-sided or narrow information database. It has been observed that:

> … better tools are available, including structural models of risks that capture cause-and-effect relationships between risk factors and outcomes (Miccolis and Shah 2001).

Supply chain risks should therefore been monitored from both the operational perspective (looking at the balance between effectiveness, efficiency, and quality) and the top-management "control" perspective (respecting the corporate governance goals and the Corporation's risk tolerance).

### Areas

Supply chain risk assessment should therefore been conducted along the key functions/processes of the supply chain.

For example, the supply chain can be broken down to areas—involving the flows and processes of the chain both inside and outside the company.

Those areas could be procurement, manufacturing, warehousing transport, and distribution.

## Objectives

Risk assessment in each area should be oriented toward the protection of the firm's strategic objectives.

Particularly in highly competitive industrial sectors, the primary supply chain objective is the creation of customer value.

This can be addressed, for example, in terms of "perfect-order index"—the critical service elements which can represent the subobjectives of the supply chain. These subobjectives are, for example: ontime deliveries; order completeness; order correctness; and damage-free and defect-free deliveries.

In many organizations, different objectives co-exist, like the goals of efficiency, quality, and customer service. Addressing the risks affecting those strategic objectives can therefore become quite complex.

For example, taking an over stock in the warehouse represents a high risk in the perspective of the efficiency, but provides a good protection against demand volatility.

For these reasons it is essential to prioritize the strategic objectives, and the individual evaluations of managers from different areas are in this sense crucial.

Each manager should identify risk factors and problems that could affect his/her job's objectives. That evaluation may be relevant in defining and prioritizing the role and importance of these objectives. Each manager will more than likely express a different perspective in that evaluation, depending on his/her job focus. As the first step, managers should define a set of "criticalities" in the achievement of these objectives.

These critical points should then be used as "drivers" in quantifying the priority of objectives and potentially, in establishing the next step, as "drivers" in risk evaluation.

At the second and third steps, managers express their comparison between these objectives. This is based on answering the question: which of the objectives is more important and how strongly?.

All the comparisons should then be checked in order to assure consistency and coherence of the evaluation. Setting up a weighted matrix for the objectives helps arriving to two key decisions: (1) defining which risks were more serious; and (2) building the priorities in managing risks.

A method that could support the prioritization of objectives is the analytic hierarchy process (AHP), developed by Saaty (1990) and applied to supply chain risk objectives by Gaudenzi and Borghesi (2006).

AHP is one of the multivariate analysis techniques that help to reduce the randomness of subjective evaluations. Its goal is to establish the "trade-off" required in complex decision-making situations, such as consideration of different objectives based on different criteria. The AHP method can be used to assess the "criticalities" affecting the strategic objectives of an organization in order to assess their importance and priority. The method requires a quantitative evaluation of the importance of each objective, compared with every other objective, and support the assessment of the weight assigned to these objectives.

**Supply Chain Risk Drivers**

Risk sources and drivers should therefore be assessed in each area particularly with a view to achieving the organization's strategic objectives.

It is preferable to select risk drivers that are measurable, objective (not based on opinions), and relevant (providing appropriate information).

The matrix of risk drivers should be described, discussed, and assessed on the basis of a shared knowledge with the managers of the different functions. This inter-functional perspective is particularly critical in the phase of evaluation, where the knowledge of individual managers allows a broader understanding of the potential impact of various risk drivers.

Thereafter the potential impact of events, and the cause–effect relationships inside the organization and along the chain, should be evaluated. Different managers have different perspectives, and these will need to be reconciled. Techniques like Delphi Method or AHP can be used during these evaluations in order to support the screening of as many factors as possible.

## 8.4 Supply Chain Risk Management Strategies

There are many sources and different studies that describe techniques and approaches for preventing and mitigating supply chain risks.

One such study, proposed by Manuj and Mentzer (2008), identified specific supply chain risk management strategies, like: avoidance, postponement, speculation, hedging, control, and sharing/transferring.

These options are often related to each other and, in many cases, the selection of one strategy can mandate the use of another one (for example, a hedging strategy entails avoiding some risks).

### *Avoidance*

Avoidance strategy is used when the risk is considered unacceptable. For example, in the case of operating in given geo-political market, or working with particular suppliers or customers or involving a high-risk technology.

In these cases, for example, managers will either divest assets or business units, or delay/renounce the entry in a given market or the collaboration with a given actor.

### *Postponement*

Postponement means delaying the actual commitment of resources to maintain flexibility and delay the incurring of costs.

The postponement facilitates the union of the leanness and agility concepts, particularly through the use of the decoupling point. As Mason-Jones et al. (1999) suggested:

> The decoupling point separates the part of the supply chain geared towards directly satisfying customer orders from the part of the supply chain based on planning. The decoupling point is also the point at which strategic stock is held as a buffer between fluctuating customer orders and/or product variety and smooth production output.

Hence, the extent of postponement and decoupling points depend on demand customization, product costs, and life cycle.

### *Speculation*

This strategy is also called assumption or selective risk taking and is the opposite of postponement. In speculation, decisions are made on anticipated customer demand. This approach is most prevalent when production is customer driven and the level of customer service is well defined and stable. In these cases, supply chain managers can allocate resources to specific customers and/or projects, depending on their value, profits margin, and cost objectives (Russo and Cardinali 2012).

### *Hedging*

In a supply-chain context, hedging is a strategy for reducing the entire supply chain risk profile. The scope is to implement specific actions in the portfolio of suppliers, customers, and facilities such that a single event (like currency fluctuations, business interruption, or a natural disaster) does not affect all the assets at the same time and/or with the same gravity.

For example, multiple sourcing can be used as a "hedge" against risks of quality, delays, disruption, or price. Maintaining two interchangeable production sites, in different locations, can be a "hedge" against risk of production shortages or increased volumes. Multiple contracting represents moreover a "hedge" to reduce variability in performance and supplier dependency.

### *Control*

Considering the multiple actors operating in the supply chain, there are evident risks related to the loss of transparency and visibility of information related to key aspects of the supply chain like products, demand, and forecasts.

Vertical integration may represent a control strategy, by reducing the risks of supply or demand failures in the supply chain, but it changes variable costs into fixed costs.

For this reason, organizations should selectively integrate those activities which can create high value, transferring less strategic activities to other firms. This strategy is called partial or tapered integration.

Similarly, in the relationships with suppliers, organizations should try to obtain the full utilization of their equipment, designing flexible contracts which consider possible changes in products/service standards, and control mechanism which might allow for some risks to be absorbed by the supplier.

### *Transferring/Sharing Risk*

The transfer and/or sharing of risks in a supply chain can be achieved through outsourcing, offshoring, and contracting to other third parties. The term "off-shoring" is typically related to global supply chains, where sourcing operates across borders.

In outsourcing and offshoring strategies there is a transfer of risk to (or sharing with) suppliers, but the collective risk of offshoring should always be evaluated for the potential impact onto the final customer, in terms of product's quality, service levels, and hence the organization's image and reputation.

Moreover, a portfolio of contracts can be used in supply chains to induce, for example, retailers with different levels of risk aversion to select unique contracts. This portfolio approach may induce the retailers in the supply chain to order quantities that maximize the expected value for the organization.

## 8.5 External contribution 8.1: What is Crisis Management?

There is a major misunderstanding between the people perception on Crisis Management and what the discipline really is. During meetings with Managers, Law Enforcement Bodies and/or Institutions, I usually spend half of the time explaining what Crisis Management does not mean rather than what it is. We need to reassure them that we do not intend to replicate what the professionals of safety and rescue are supposed to do and that we are not going to get in their way in case of an adverse event. The sooner we resolve this issue, the better it is for our

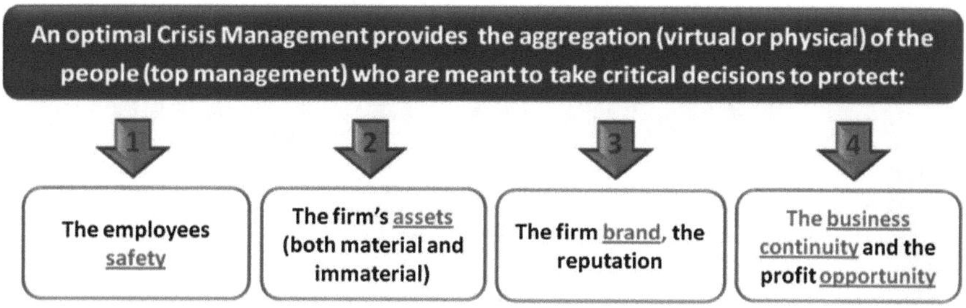


**Fig. 8.2** Critical decisions in crisis management

mission. If it becomes clear what we do not want to do and what we definitely do not represent, we can finally clarify to everyone the added value of our support and the importance of our objectives. The perception we are fighting is that crisis management is about the ability to react to a Crisis wrong. That is why the law enforcement and the institutions become nervous, as they are the champions of such an activity, they have the skills and the resources and no one can do it better. Crisis Management is really about the ability to get ready, be prepared to any kind of event, and it is the first step of a process. In fact, the firms, who practice it at a good level, achieve the invocation of business continuity as fast as possible. In a major incident, no one looks after the continuity of the business as a top priority. The focus, as shown in the graph below, is always on people safety, on the assets (material and immaterial) to be safeguarded, the reputation (through communication) to be protected, and lastly the business continuity (Fig. 8.2).

A firm excels in Crisis Management when it is able to reach the fourth priority very quickly as the survival of the business comes afterward, but at the same time is imperative to comply with the absolute concept that a crisis cannot be declared resolved until a complete return to normality (and if the business does not survive, there is an even worst consequential crisis). The methodology in crisis management drives a firm through the right decisions to be taken to reach the fourth objective.

Crisis Management, therefore, is all about *prevention*. Especially, in Italy we need to improve a lot as we do not excel at that, while we too often get pride in how keen and skilled are at improvising and reacting promptly and smartly at any event.

Crisis Management is a discipline that has tools, methodologies, and protocols. It is very valuable in any firm who wishes to demonstrate concrete responsibility toward the ethics they often forget, i.e. the care for human resources working in their environment, staff being their most precious asset, the centrality of the human being and so on and so forth. I wonder how they can really respect their own words if they do not practice a robust Crisis Management. I always refer to Crisis Management as *the art to make decisions*.

While Business Continuity is often confused with Disaster Recovery and it is still very much exercised as a technological event, it should be clear to everyone

| | Technology | Business | Executive Management |
|---|---|---|---|
| Process | Disaster Recovery | Business Continuity | Crisis Management |
| Activity | Data back up /mirroring on line<br>High technology alternative rooms<br>Recovery desks<br>Back up | The business participates more actively to tests, analysing its own critical processes and identifies the most critical resources<br>Each line of busines invests in the Business Continuity | In a crisis the Managers follow a predefined protocol which is coordinated by the Crisis Management team<br>The decision to invoke Business Continuity and Disaster Recovery are taken rapidly. More focus on people safety. |
| Methodology | Duplication of the Data Center (big Companies)<br>Rental of Data Centers (small/medium Companies)<br>Remote archiving of tapes<br>Telecommunication investments | Business Impact Analysis<br>Definition of "RTOs - recovery time objectives"<br>Definition of "RPOs - recovery point objectives"<br>Business Continuity Plans | "Calling tree" and evacuation plans<br>Crisis Plans with roles and responsibilities predefined by Top Management<br>Test providing a simulation of Crisis Scenarios |

**Fig. 8.3** Disaster recovery, business continuity, and crisis management

that crisis management is a top management event, as it enables a firm to gather, virtually and physically, the executive team who needs to reach concurrence on vital and difficult actions in the most efficient way, possibly in a critical situations, i.e. even without the comfort of intelligent information they still have to make intelligent decisions (Fig. 8.3).

## *The Situation "As Is" and How to Improve Crisis Management*

There are very few firms practicing Crisis Management as it should be. Often people tell me they do have Crisis Management because they rent a space to recover their technology. Disaster Recovery and Business Continuity often get confused with Crisis Management. Among the companies that do practice Crisis Management, there are a few critical infrastructures who invested significant money in building a crisis room where they gather the executive team in case of major events. Other firms have started exercising Crisis simulations. This test is usually named "table top", as the whole event is played around a meeting table, and it is based on intellectual interaction, simulating a crisis. It is a most effective exercise as it is a deep training session, and it shows efficiently the gaps to be resolved and the possible lack of communication among the members of the team.

Many firms have developed a Crisis Plan and few firms have even created a Pandemic Plan. However, what I observe in most of the cases, Crisis Management criteria are not fully followed and I will enlist just few examples that could be useful to improve the activities of Crisis Management:

1. Evacuation tests are rarely performed in a professional manner: first of all they should never be preannounced. In addition, the Security Managers often complain that there are always employees, especially among the Top Managers, who refuse to leave the building. This is totally unacceptable as any security norm does not have a chance to be respected if the good example does not start from the Top. There are many other ways to avoid disruption to the business, but the date and time of an evacuation test should be agreed and known by the minimum number of people.
2. Preparation should be both at the central and local level: big multinational companies hold plans, perform test, and train people just within their headquarters. This is not enough, as it is important to be ready to face a crisis at the local level. Even the most powerful Crisis Management engine will not be able to reach and aid those in difficulty in the first few hours and the time right after an event is really vital. Anyone at any level in any location should be enabled to make decisions and act independently.
3. Sometime "invacuation" rather than "evacuation" is to be suggested. In situations like flooding or other risks (bombs) in the perimeter outside the building, people safety implies that invacuation is better and all the staff should aggregate at the center of the building as far away as possible from windows. Firms need to train staff on it well before an event occurs otherwise there is no chance that the employees will listen and stay inside.
4. Companies should demand the same level of resilience to all their stakeholders. If the wider scenario is not considered, it is probable that the weakness of one exposes everyone else. There is a lot of debate on the domino effect of a potential crisis. In the globalized world this issue has reached a significance that goes beyond the will to defend the boarders, the national identities and the local practices. The financial crises have revealed the vulnerabilities of many for the malpractice of few. In Crisis Management, we have to understand that we need to demand the same kind of preparedness to all the stakeholders in order to guarantee our own survival.

## *The Best Laid Plan: Communication*

The most important tool to mitigate the consequences of a crisis is communication. The Crisis communication plan has to be the strongest, it needs to be prepared and concurred well before an event and any firm has to agree on the role of the spokesperson, internal or external, who will represent the company perspective. This cannot be improvised. Top Managers, even those who are communicating daily with journalists on technical or financial aspects, may fail dangerously in communicating on soft or environmental issues. Bad communication does often worsen the effects as the most valuable asset of a company is its reputation. As we know, we learn much more from our mistakes rather than from our successes; however, the smartest professionals study and analyze others' mistakes and take advantage from the adverse luck of their competitors well before they have to learn from direct experience. One of the examples of poor communication in the past few years has been the BP oil spill in the Gulf of Mexico. The CEO denial of responsibility (not our drill, not our equipment, not our resources) did not help, as well as the under evaluation of how his British accent was being received in a location where Southern American is spoken. The last unforgivable mistake he made was the attempt to attract empathy for being exhausted and wishing to get his life back (in a disaster where many people lost their job and significant environmental impact had damaged the country for a long time).

Communicating well is the ultimate defense and cannot be failed. The evolving era we are living tells us that we need to adjust to the technological changes quickly. For example, there is no chance that a lie or a half-truth can survive few hours. There is always someone witnessing, filming, taking pictures, recording, and catching the liars unaware. The propagation of news, true or false, right, or wrong, goes around at light speed through the social networks. Who is still monitoring just the traditional media is missing a world of potential slanders or misrepresentation of our problems that could damage the reputation gained by a company in ages of good work and strenuous efforts.

## Conclusion

In Italy we take pride to be the best rescuers in the world. Our ability to improvise, our wisdom, our courage in crises is cited everywhere and sufficiently self appraised any time we live a nightmare, whether it is a natural catastrophe or a terroristic attack. I am willing to join the club of people who believes that our ability in reaction is mythical if we are finally able to recognize and admit that our inability in prevention is as much as legendary. And we should not be proud of it. Italians need to be heroes of reaction, because we are totally inefficient in preventing disaster. Our culture drives us to fatalism not to realism and we forget quickly the painful cost of such a behavior.

I would willingly swap the flattering compliments of being foxy, smart, and acute in rapid actions with the recognition of wisdom, professionalism, defining preventative plans, and foreseeing solutions. Sometimes our ability to react can only be exercised in counting the victims or indicating faults and negligence in court rooms.

## *Author Profile*

Gianna Detoni is the founder and Managing Director of Panta Ray and Chairman of the HI CARE Foundation. Milanese, she is among the leading experts in international techniques of business management and risk resiliency thanks to her experience of over 30 years in a leading international bank. Gianna is one of the few figures in Italy with internationally recognized certifications as Certified Business Continuity Professional (CBCP) with the Disaster Recovery Institute and Master Business Continuity Institute (MBCI). Recently, she has been given the task to contribute to the new edition of the Good Practice Guidelines of the BCI and will be listed as one of the authors. After covering important international roles in the J.P.Morgan Chase Bank, including Technology & Operations Manager, EMEA Resiliency Risk Manager, Operational Risk Manager since 2007 assumed the role of International Crisis Manager for Europe, Middle East and Africa within the function of Corporate Security and Investigation. In 2009, Gianna founded Panta Ray and created the Crisis and Fraud Management program to offer know-how and methodologies to companies and institutions. Since 2010 she is Chairman of HI CARE–Human & Infrastructure Crisis in Emergency Aid & Rescue (www.hi-care.eu), a network of Companies that proactively share the difficulties of Security and Crisis Management in the city.

## 8.6 External contribution 8.2: Disaster Recovery for Industrial Plant: Manufacturing Industry

Restoration is an emergency service, following a loss incident like fire, flood, or storm damage. Contrary to other emergency services, restoration is not yet well known by the public. Restoration has the objective to support a person or an organization suffering a loss after such an incident and to provide service creating "pre-disaster" conditions as soon as possible.

In case of commercial or industrial losses, a highly specialized know-how in decontamination techniques, as well as repair and project management, fast applied, reduces the business interruption and the potential or real loss of market. Consequential losses in case of interdependency of production and services are reduced as well. In any case, restoration as a type of repair service has a higher value compared with the purchase of new equipment.

For buildings the restoration work is mainly decontamination, drying, and to a certain degree repair/renovation work. Equipment usually undergoes a process of special decontamination, drying, and repair in case of need.

Professional restoration offers a "full service" approach to the customer, including technical expertise as well as the coordination between different tasks.

Very often service departments of OEM and maintenance specialists are not aware of the possibilities and prospects of restoration; on the contrary, they often favor the delivery of new equipment.

However, as fire thermally damaged equipment cannot be restored, restoration deals with the contamination by soot, fire extinguishing powder, water (white = fresh, grey = slightly contaminated or black = contaminated with mud), hydrochloric acid, and in case of technical dysfunctions with spills of other chemicals.

## *The Case: Fire in a Semiconductor Plant*

The customer drives a semiconductor plant with some 1,100 employees for production, research, and development. The product has been 5″ wafers for chips used in TV-tuners, mobile radios, and specific customized integrated circuits in small numbers for different customers. In 2001, this plant was downsized to the above mentioned size.

A fire broke out on December 12, 2003 and destroyed not only the roof but also some equipment and structure of the production which was under clean room conditions.

In these buildings, clean room installations and production tools for the semiconductors with a value of more than several € 100 million had been operating. The loss resulting from the damage was soon estimated to exceed € 100 million, business interruption not included. Some even saw the whole factory at risk as in case of such a damage the transfer to another place or even country is an option.

The customer called BELFOR during the incident as, due to prior damages where restoration was used with success, he was aware of the possibilities and benefits of restoration and in the disaster planning a possible restoration was included. Further in some countries he is partner in the Red Alert® pre-disaster program.

The first meeting on site happened the same evening, Friday December 12th (Fig. 8.4).

## *The Restoration Project—First Intervention*

After a quick inspection and evaluation first intervention measures were started.

To stop the further progress of damage during the weekend the water was removed from the floor and separations were built to reduce the spread of contamination throughout the buildings. With heavy drying equipment (some 15 adsorption dehumidifiers) the relative humidity was soon reduced below 35 % and kept under this critical level in areas with equipment where a chance for restoration was given.

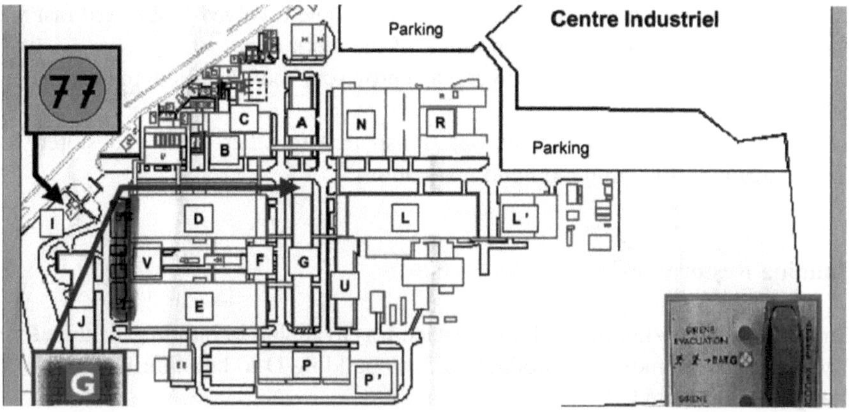


**Fig. 8.4** The layout of the plant

In the first days after the fire a detailed inspection was carried out and proposals for further restoration of buildings, technical installations, and equipment were submitted.

## *The Restoration*

Like usual a huge number of parties were involved, besides BELFOR:

- customer holding for strategic decisions;
- loss adjuster from two countries;
- customer's risk managers;
- customer's plant manager and technical managers;
- UK investigation agency for damage investigation;
- forensic accountants from the UK and US for financial control;
- insurers and re-insurers from all over the world.

## *Experience Capacity Key Success Factors*

After agreement with the customer on a restoration project an international restoration team was formed and arrived on site. BELFOR specialists from France, the Netherlands, Germany, UK, Belgium and Switzerland were included, as well as some people from the BELFOR International Technical Support division (Munich, Germany).

As typical for such projects, the number of people involved first raised fast and was reduced then following the progress of the work done.

One of the first measures was to create a provisory roof to protect the equipment below against the weather.

However, movable equipment was transported to other areas and stored for further treatment (examination and restoration).

### Building Restoration

Due to the downsizing in 2001 some space was available in building E; therefore, it was possible to move the production from building D to building E, which was "only" contaminated.

The restoration work started in the building M on December 18th. Soon afterwards, the decontamination of building E was started as well. Priority was given to the air conditioning and air supply system as well as to the other media supply systems.

Stainless steel media lines also showed corrosion due to the chloride contamination. Such contamination leads to the risk of pitting. Therefore, such pipes with media under pressure have not been restored but replaced.

Decontamination work in such an environment is very complex and needs "artistic" skills, apart from knowledge and experience in dealing with soot, hydrochloric acid, and other fire-related contamination.

The work in building E and M was finished by the end of January. Building V was decontaminated on February 7th. The customer reconditioned the clean room in building E starting on February 2nd.

Therefore, it was possible to start with the installation of the tools in mid-February. Production was restarted 10 weeks after the fire. Building D was demolished as it had been too heavily damaged by the fire.

### Restoration of Production Tools and Other Equipment

All equipment which had been previously secured was inspected and the options for restoration were evaluated. The customer decided which tools he would need for future use. These were then restored based on a priority list defined by the customer.

The restoration procedure covered mainly the following steps:

- dismantling;
- decontamination;
- montage;
- transport to a pre clean room;
- clean room decontamination;
- transport to the real clean room;

- final wipe down;
- final test.

There is a lack of standards concerning the acceptable amounts of remaining contamination for clean room conditions. Therefore, there was a discussion together with the client about the degree of remaining conductive or corrosive contamination. Following the former MIL and the currently widely accepted Joint-Industry Standards, the target for the restoration work on all the electronic, optical and mechanic devices, and machines was defined.

Functionality tests were performed including the manufacturer, the tool technicians, and BELFOR staff in order to find any failures and its sources immediately as the time frame for finalizing the restoration work was exactly defined and should not be exceeded.

To ensure the high level of cleanliness and reliability for the restored equipment, special care was given to a specially adapted quality management: all the agreements with the client on priorities, the cleanliness, and documentation of each step as well as each single step of cleaning, intermediate quality checks till the final reassembly were documented and taught to the technicians during a jour fix for every shift. Discrepancies were communicated from one shift to the next and published in so-called Quality News in order to ensure the necessary improvement.

Some 1,300 items have been restored. This includes:

- ASML Wafer steppers or Applied Material ion implanters;
- wet benches;
- etchers CVD Systems;
- dry(gas) and wet etchers;
- different lithographic systems;
- defective measurement system;
- 17 vacuum pump systems;
- microscopes and a lot of others.

The restored equipment has a replacement value of some € 70 million. The restoration cost is some 3 %(!). Some other equipment which could be restored was scrapped due to the fact that the technology was outdated and this equipment was not needed for future production. Production could start as planned and until today–more than six months after start up in the new clean room—no complications have been reported.

## *General Survey of the Cost*

Total Cost of Restoration ~6,950 k€

Building: Decontamination/Restoration 23 %

Decontamination of Air ducts and aggregates 14 %

**Table 8.1** Actions plan

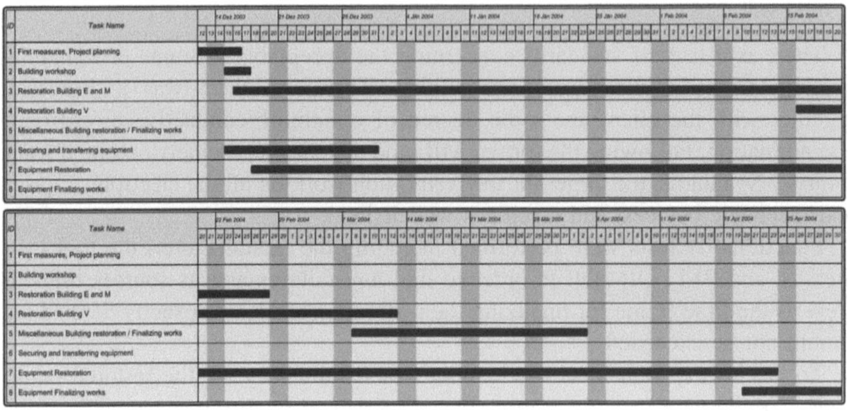


Equipment: Drying 3 %
Decontamination/Restoration 20 %
Workshop 9 %
Not assigned: Travel and Lodging 13 %
Overtime 12 %
Logistic and Transport 6 %

## *Conclusion*

Restoration helps to overcome a critical situation following an incident like fire water or contamination faster. Therefore it reduces business interruption, consequential losses, and the property loss. In the case above major savings (>90 %) could be achieved. This is a typical result in case of fire damage in the industry. In addition employment and presence on the market was secured.

Restoration is more efficient if started immediately respectively as soon as possible. Restoration planning as a part of any business continuity planning is a high value in case of disaster. This has become clearly evident in the described case and is recommended for a state-of-the-art business continuity planning (Table 8.1).

## *Corporate Profile*

BELFOR is worldwide leader in disaster recovery and property restoration. A global partner for insurers, brokers, and corporate to reduce losses after fire, flood, storm, on buildings, inventory, machinery, electronics, documents, and other goods.

With more than 5,500 employees in 260 offices spanning 30 countries BELFOR provides professional services 24 h a day 365 days a year.

Through its international network BELFOR can reach any incident site in the world at very short notice and, in most cases, intervene and initiate action to stabilize the situation within the first 24–48 h from the damage. For more info: www.belfor.com.

## References


Bowersox DJ, Daugherty PJ (1995) Logistics paradigms: the impact of information technology. J Bus Logist 16(1):65–80

Christopher M (1998) Logistics & supply chain management: strategies for reducing cost and improving services, 2nd edn. Financial Times Prentice-Hall, New York

Christopher M (2003) Understanding supply chain risk. Cranfield University, Cranfield

Christopher M (2004) Identifying and managing supply chain vulnerability. www.iolt.org.uk

Croxton KL, Garcìa-Dastugue SJ, Lambert DM, Rogers DS (2001) The supply chain management processes. Int J Logist Manag 12(2):13–36

Gardner JT, Cooper MC (2003) Strategic supply chain mapping approaches. J Bus Logist. 24(2):37–64

Gaudenzi B, Borghesi A (2006) Managing risks in the supply chain using the AHP method. Int J Logist Manag 17(1):114–136

Holfmann E (2010) Linking corporate strategy and supply chain management. Int J Phys Distrib Logist Manage 40(4):256–276

Jüttner U, Peck H, Christopher M (2003) Supply chain risk management: outlining an agenda for future research. Int J Logist: Res Appl 6(4):197–210

Manuj I, Mentzer JT (2008) Global supply chain risk management. J Bus Logist 29(1):133–155

Mason-Jones R, Naylor B, Towill DR (1999) Engineering the leagile supply chain. Int J Agile Manag Syst 2(1):54–61

Miccolis J, Shah S (2001) Modelling the reality of risk: the cornerstone of ERM, expert commentary. www.irmi.com

Russo I, Cardinali S (2012) Product returns and customer value. In: Jodlbauer H (ed) A footware industry case in modelling value, contributions to management science, Part 2, pp 79–97

Saaty TL (1990) The analytic hierarchy process. RWS Publications, Shallowater

Zsidisin GA (2004) An analysis of supply chain risk assessment techniques. Int J Phys Distrib Logist Manag 34(5):397–413

MIX
Papier aus verantwortungsvollen Quellen
Paper from responsible sources
FSC® C105338

If you have any concerns about our products,
you can contact us on
**ProductSafety@springernature.com**

In case Publisher is established outside the EU,
the EU authorized representative is:
**Springer Nature Customer Service Center GmbH**
**Europaplatz 3, 69115 Heidelberg, Germany**

Printed by Libri Plureos GmbH
in Hamburg, Germany